THE ADVENTURE SERIES
SAILING

THE ADVENTURE SERIES
SAILING
ANNEKA RICE

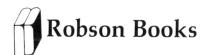 Robson Books

Drawings by Harold King

First published in Great Britain in 1988 by Robson Books Ltd,
Bolsover House, 5–6 Clipstone Street, London W1P 7EB.

British Library Cataloguing in Publication Data

Rice, Anneka
   Sailing.——(The Adventure series).
   1. Sailing
   I. Title   II. Series
   797.1'24   GV811

ISBN 0-86051-462-5

Typeset by AKM Associates (UK) Ltd,
Ajmal House, Hayes Road, Southall, London

Printed in Great Britain by St Edmundsbury Press Ltd, Bury
St Edmunds, Suffolk

Bound by Dorstel Press Ltd, Harlow, Essex

Acknowledgements

Many people have helped me to learn to sail and to put this book together. Ray Robinson was the photographer, Nancy Duin did a great deal of additional research and Janice Broxup's legendary enthusiasm made it all happen on time. I would also like to thank the Royal Yachting Association for all the help and encouragement received and, of course, everyone at Plas Menai for their patience and hospitality.

Also, a special thank you to Mike whose plans for a quiet holiday in Wales went somewhat awry!

Foreword

Welcome to the sport of sailing!

Sailing is now one of the most popular participant sports in Britain. The progress of a normal beginner's course is charted in this book, although with her usual enthusiasm, Anneka managed to instil a certain amount of chaos into the week! However, like thousands of other people every year, she found that the basic techniques of dinghy handling can be learned quickly and easily, provided you have the right training.

This means learning at a school, club or centre recognized by the Royal Yachting Association. I'm glad that, when the Adventure Series was being planned, Anneka took my advice and experienced the rugged beauty and challenging environment of Plas Menai.

You don't have to be as agile as Annie to enjoy sailing. While it's true that some children start at the age of five or six, other people are only introduced to the sport as a retirement hobby. Perhaps that's one of the great attractions of sailing: unlike some other recreational activities, you can choose your own pace – and the class of boat you sail – to suit your involvement . . . and you won't be condemned as a 'veteran' when you pass your 30th birthday!

Whether you're looking for the freedom to explore our coasts or seeking the challenge of competitive sport at the highest level, sailing will have something to offer – as a sport for life. Annie herself puts it so well when she says: 'If you miss out on sailing, you're really missing out on one of the great adventure sports. Don't forget, it's your turn next!'

Good sailing!

John Driscoll
RYA National Sailing Coach

Introduction

I'm rather embarassed to admit that, until recently, I couldn't sail, despite having been on boats all my life.

When I was a child, my summer holidays were spent at Seaview on the Isle of Wight – a sailing village teeming with yellow sou'westers and squeaking oilskins, the seafront dotted with dinghies and small children like Michelin men, squeezed into huge life jackets. I was one of those small children; but somehow I was drawn to the beach, where I'd discovered something far more absorbing: sandcastles.

Perhaps the word 'sandcastle' is misleading – these were works of art, sculptures, amazing feats of architecture. I blame a chap called Peter Terry. His golf-ball runs were masterpieces of engineering – and while there were tunnels to scoop out, bridges to build and moats to fill with water, I was landlocked.

When a boat trip became unavoidable I obediently pulled on my bit of rope when called upon. However it was always a mystery to me that we ever got the boat moving at all, ploughing through swimmers, lilos and waterwings.

I remember one hapless journey with a seasoned seadog of about ten – my friend Jamie. We sailed off to buy ice creams at the yacht club, ignoring the armada of yachts bearing down on us from the opposite direction. Puzzled by the cries and gesticulations, we eventually reached the jetty to discover that we'd ruined the start of an important race. My father cringed into his guernsey as irate yachtsmen barked, 'Who do those children belong to?'

So, sailing was not for me as a child, and my shaky start remained shaky. I've since been on boats everywhere from the Great Barrier Reef to Frensham Ponds, and I've managed to pull in my bit of rope with great aplomb – but I've never learned how to take charge. Secretly, I've longed to know what it is about the sport that obsesses such a large percentage of the population.

Day 1

As we set off for Wales, I felt a wave of nostalgia for those childhood summer holidays, with the car packed to the roof with the ridiculous range of gear you need for British summers: everything from anoraks, umbrellas and snorkels to buckets, spades and Monopoly. This time, we'd brought a bucket, too, though I think this was more for the benefit of Trevor – Ray's faithful, smelly but lovable four-legged friend.

We were bound for the northwestern tip of Wales, just across the Menai Strait from the island of Anglesey. The long journey there took us through staggeringly beautiful scenery: huge, shadowy mountains sinking into deep, still lakes. The closer we got to our destination, the slower we went as we negotiated tortuous passes and pretty stone bridges cupped over tiny gushing streams. The villages we slipped past seemed to belong to a different age, and as dusk approached, we could barely distinguish the old dark-stone cottages from the boulders and rocky hillsides nearby. Luckily, my Aussie photographer friend, Ray, demonstrated outstanding orienteering talents – or was he just gasping for some cool, clear amber nectar?

Suddenly we turned off the main road into a little lane and then screeched to a halt by a sign hewn into a rock by the side of a large, modern stone building. This was it: Plas Menai, the National Watersports Centre of Wales – or *Canolfan Cenedlaethol Chwaraeon Dŵr Cymru*, as it des-

The Royal Yachting Association

In 1875, there were 49 yacht clubs in the British Isles, but no overall authority to produce national racing rules. As a result, a meeting was called at the Willis Rooms in St James's, London, chaired by the Marquis of Exeter, who was also the Commodore of the Royal Victoria Yacht Club at Ryde on the Isle of Wight. That night, the Yacht Racing Assocation (YRA) was founded, with the Marquis as its first president.

By the 1940s, however, there were calls for the formation of an organization that would represent all national yachting interests - from

Day 1 continued

cribed itself on the rock. For the next week this was going to be home, and where I was going to learn to sail.

. There *must* be something in the fact that the British Isles are surrounded by water because I've definitely got the sea in my blood. I love the wind-in-the-hair syndrome, the bracing bite of the spray, the crash of the waves, not to mention the tot of rum. Now, at last, I had the opportunity to throw myself against the elements and learn how to master them.

When we sat down to map out the Adventure Series, learning how to sail (and being filmed doing it) was number one on my list – and my number one place to learn was Plas Menai. This, I'd been reliably informed by the Royal Yachting Association, is the best-equipped national sailing centre in Britain, and its principal is former national sailing coach

Bob Bond. I'd encountered both Plas Menai and Bob a few years ago when we did a *Treasure Hunt* in the area – he'd fished me out of the Menai Strait after one of my obligatory dunkings from a helicopter. I reckoned that he was the man for the job.

Plas Menai's setting is certainly impressive. The Centre is relatively new (it was built by the Sports Council for Wales only in 1983), but it blends in with the spectacular Snowdonia countryside of mountains and water. It's also surprisingly large, with accommodation for up to 90 people as well as lecture rooms, a laboratory and darkroom, its own boatyard and even an indoor pool.

Although my course didn't actually start until Monday, the new intakes had to arrive on Sunday evening so that we could get settled in, ready for an early start the next day. As Ray and I clattered into the foyer, dropping

small dinghy sailing to motor yachting – and the YRA finally changed its name to the Yachting Association in 1952 to reflect the expansion of its duties. The following year, it was granted permission to add 'Royal' before its name.

In 1952, the then YA had 650 clubs and 2100 private individuals as members. Today, there are more than 1400 RYA-affiliated clubs and about 65,000 personal members. By 1972, it had introduced a national proficiency scheme and a national association of schools sailing, and it now offers training for dinghy sailors, sportsboat enthusiasts, those keen on cruising (up to 'yachtmaster' level) and windsurfers. Its publications and

Boats skim over the waves in front of the Plas Menai sailing centre.
Looks easy, doesn't it?

enquiry service are extensions of this educational role.

The RYA is not only concerned with training, however. It still manages national and international (including Olympic) yacht and powerboat racing, devising rules and appeal procedures, organizing coaching and selection, and even measuring craft to make sure that they qualify for various racing events. It maintains contacts with local and national government, both to advise them and to protect members' interests; it also performs these functions on the international stage. Boat construction, safety standards, club liability and weather forecasts are only a few of the areas on which the RYA can give advice.

Day 1 continued

our luggage on the slate floor, we discovered that reception was closed for the night. A note directed us to the bar – what a civilized place! – where we soon made contact with Paul Dufton, one of the instructors, who was making himself known to the new recruits, who had come to Plas Menai from all over Britain.

Paul directed us to our rooms, which were small, pine-panelled and Nordic-looking, each with its own shower. On each door, there was a list of house rules – 'Make your own bed . . . Don't be late for meals . . .' (what time's assembly and extra games?). The best thing was that there were no telephones in the rooms – and the Snowdonian mountains were to prove too much for my mobile phone. Escape at last!

The next hour was spent rushing in and out of each other's rooms comparing views, rules and who had the luxury of a mirror on their wall. The views were stunning, right over the Menai Strait across to the dusky silhouette of Anglesey beyond. By now, the sun had sunk behind the hills, washing the sea and craggy rocks with the slate grey of evening shadows.

Trevor wasn't too impressed with the kennel facilities: basically, there weren't any! Dogs are not allowed at the Centre, so poor Trevor was smuggled out to the garages in the yard.

I was desperate to go for a swim after that long drive. However, the Centre's large indoor pool was mysteriously screened off, with 'NO ENTRY' signs on the doors. I was about to burst in when Paul arrived and explained that it was at my peril: the North Wales Naturist Club had booked in for the evening, but I was very welcome to join them. I was gripped with indecision for about three seconds, then sloped

The Menai Strait is a navigable waterway that separates Anglesey from the Welsh mainland. It is approximately 10 miles in length. The Strait is relatively narrow – in places less than 300 yards across.

Day 1 continued

off to the bar.

The noise level was deafening, everyone enthusing about the pleasures and adventures to come the following week. Plas Menai isn't only about sailing, although that's what it's best known for: some of those in the bar had signed up to learn canoeing, windsurfing, sub-aqua diving, waterskiing, mountain walking and climbing. And there wasn't just one type of sailing on offer – there was a choice between cruising, power boating and shore-based courses on sailing theory, as well as the dinghy sailing course that I would be taking.

Everyone was cheerfully barracking each other about the courses they were going to do – the windsurfers, lean and hungry-looking, mean and moody, claiming to be the 'real men' because they were about to embark on such a gruelling course, unlike us pampered, gin-swilling sailors lounging in our luxurious yachts. Ha! (For the *real* story, turn these pages and read on.)

It was getting late, and I still had all my unpacking to do. I returned to my room, and as I opened my suitcase, a piece of yellow paper fluttered to the floor. This was the course information sheet, sent to me in advance and containing a checklist of what to bring, from first aid kits to whistles and thermos flasks. You really can't be too prepared for sailing. You never know what the weather's going to be like, or how much time you're going to be spending hanging around in the damp cold outside or, for that matter, in the water.

And later in the week I was to discover how very windy and exposed it can be on the sea – no matter how warmly I dressed. Sailing is an invigorating and hardy sport, and you really can't enjoy it when you're wet and miserable.

Plas Menai would provide us all with life jackets or buoyancy aids, and waterproofs and wetsuits if we needed them. For our feet, they recommended trainers, though I didn't fancy wading around in soggy plimsolls all week. So instead, I'd brought along my scuba-diving boots. For the rest of the week, my feet stayed warm and dry and the boots remained in one piece, while I watched the rest of my class's footwear gradually disintegrate.

The others on my course seemed a lovely bunch of people, the film crew were cheerful and eager to get going and the atmosphere at the Centre seemed happy, relaxed but business-like.

There was a lot of whooping and laughing coming from the pool area – maybe I should have had that swim after all.

DAY 2

Waking up took me back to boarding school days (or, rather what I imagined them to be as I never went to one): endless feet running up and down corridors, doors slamming and plumbing screeching and whining all around. I tried ignoring it all until the sounds began to die down and it was a more civilized time of the morning. Breakfast

The view across the Strait from my room

Life jackets and buoyancy aids

Everyone venturing on to the water must wear some kind of life-saving gear in case of an accident or simply to give you that vital margin of safety when practising such things as capsize drills. On all sailing courses, at home and abroad, you will be provided with one of the two types: life jackets and buoyancy aids.

Life jackets are familiar to most of us. Fitting around the neck like a horse's collar and extending down the front of the chest, they are known to Americans as 'Mae Wests', for obvious reasons! When fully

15

Day 2 continued

at Plas Menai is at 8.00 am *sharp*, but judging by the savoury smells wafting up from the dining room, it was a bit too serious for me.

It was a lovely, bright day, and the view out of my window across the Menai Strait was a real reviver. We were surrounded by rolling green hills that swept down to a stretch of glistening water that looked much more like a wide river than an arm of the sea.

Dressing proved a bit of a problem. I wasn't sure if we'd be going straight out on the water or would be stuck on land for our first lesson. To be on the safe side, I lugged my wetsuit and boots down to the locker rooms in the Centre's basement, near the quayside, and then went off to look for the others in my class.

By the time I got to the dining room, everyone had finished eating and was fully occupied with making lunch. This was an art form in itself. One table was covered with a great, groaning spread of bread, cheese, boiled eggs, pickle, tunafish and lots of other fillings. It was down to each individual to make up their own packed lunch. This really *was* like school, particularly the standard-issue bag of crisps and apple.

In all, there were about 30 people starting classes that day, divided into three roughly equal groups that would each be learning something different. Those on the dinghy sailing course were asked to assemble outside in the sunshine. There were 11 of us. Maureen and the very nautical-looking Bob from Ashford in Kent were very keen to learn, having already decided that they

Opposite
Kitted up, ready to go
Overleaf
With Bob Bond and Mike *and* rigging the boat

inflated, they ensure that an unconscious person will float face upwards so that breathing won't be impaired. Some types have to be filled by blowing down a tube; others are filled automatically or semi-automatically via a gas cylinder. The best are those conforming to the British Standard 3595, marked with a 'kitemark'.

Unfortunately, life jackets are ·fairly clumsy to wear and can get in the way if you are constantly moving around, as you are when you're sailing. Instead, you can use a *buoyancy aid*. Resembling a padded waistcoat, this will provide you with enough buoyancy to stay on top of the water, although it isn't as safe as a life jacket. For this reason,

Day 2 continued

The raw recruits are met by Bob

Opposite
Sailing – and capsized

buoyancy aids should only be worn in sheltered or inshore waters. The best types are the ones approved by the British Marine Industries Federation.

At high water during a spring tide, the tidal stream in the Menai Strait is generally 3 knots in the wider parts, but increases to 8 knots in The Swellies (*see page 97*).

wanted to buy their own boat even before they'd had a day's sailing. Sandy and her teenage son James had travelled from their home in Clwyd, and there was also a family from Gwent: David with his two sons Job and Dave, and Dave's girlfriend Siân. David had signed up because it was an opportunity to have a holiday involving both his sons; if it were a success, they would go sailing together again.

Finally there was Mike, an architect from Macclesfield, and his 9-year-old son Tom. As with everyone else, this was a bit of a trial run: if Tom really liked sailing, they might get a boat in the future. Tom was a bit young for

There they are, just waiting for us

Opposite
The kit!

Day 2 continued

Day 2 continued

learning in a Wayfarer – children of his age are usually taught to sail in the much smaller Optimists and Toppers – but Mike really wanted them to have a holiday together doing the same things.

Tom was to prove a source of inspiration to us all that week – open, bright and questioning. When he saw me joining his class, he cut right through all the great British reserve by yelling out, 'Cor, that's Anneka Rice!' so loudly that his voice echoed round the entire Centre. I shrank into the shadows with embarrassment. But Tom was to become a great buddy, his spontaneity and directness two of the highlights of the week.

There was a very jolly family

**'This is a boat.'
Bob starts with the basics**

atmosphere as we waited for our instructors. Our chat died away as the principal of Plas Menai (and former RYA National Coach), Bob Bond, arrived, smiling and full of charm. Bob told us that, before we could meet our instructors or even see the boats we'd be sailing in, we had to be dressed properly. You might not think that you need much kit for sailing, but for safety's sake, you

Opposite
The parts of a boat

24

Parts of the sails

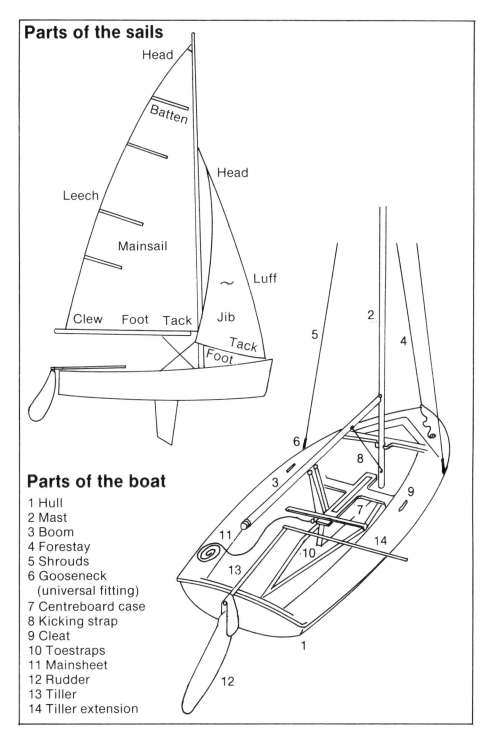

Head
Batten
Head
Leech
Mainsail
Luff
Clew   Foot   Tack   Jib
Tack
Foot

Parts of the boat

1 Hull
2 Mast
3 Boom
4 Forestay
5 Shrouds
6 Gooseneck
   (universal fitting)
7 Centreboard case
8 Kicking strap
9 Cleat
10 Toestraps
11 Mainsheet
12 Rudder
13 Tiller
14 Tiller extension

Day 2 continued

have to have some sort of life jacket. Because the weather can turn cold – and because it is usually a lot colder on (not to mention *in*) the water – some protective clothing is also in order.

Bob led us to the storeroom, where there were rows and rows of nylon waterproofs, wet suits, buoyancy aids and life jackets (*see box*). Not surprisingly, considering how many hundreds of pieces of equipment the storekeeper had to keep tabs on, everything was handed out in a very orderly fashion. Each class was dealt with in turn, the storekeeper checking out the necessary bits of protective clothing (complete with identifying codes) to each student, with directions as to which particular rails they should be returned at the end of the day, once they had been rinsed out – a real military operation. I collected a buoyancy aid and some waterproofs and deposited these with my wetsuit and boots in the locker room.

I joined the rest of the class down on the quayside where Bob was waiting for us beside a row of innocent-looking yellow and white boats. These were Wayfarers – according to Bob, good, general-purpose family boats that are easy to learn to sail and supposedly very stable.

Bob gathered us round one of the Wayfarers and, very painstakingly, showed us each element of rigging a boat. Everyone seemed to be nodding sagely as he took us on a guided tour of the boat, describing each shank, sheet and shackle. I felt a sense of rising panic . . . cheats, all of them! They've sailed before! I hated them all as they showed not the slightest sign of bewilderment – not a flush, not a bead of sweat. It was only later I found out that they all felt as desperate as I did – but, with the video camera pointing up their noses, they decide that the calm, totally-in-control look would further their TV careers better.

'We'll start by attaching the large sail, which is called the mainsail,' said Bob, pronouncing it 'main-sul', and taking hold of

Opposite
Bob shows the class how to rig the boat

It is quite easy to see why a boat sails when the wind is behind it and pushes it forward, but how does it sail forward when the wind is coming from the side or in front?

When the wind comes from these directions, the boat's centreboard (or a deep keel) discourages it from moving sideways. And because of this, the energy exerted by the wind will take the line of least resistance and be converted into forward movement.

Day 2 continued

the largest piece of stiff white cloth. 'This goes on to the piece of metal that you'll become very familiar with during the week. It's the one that normally spends its time swinging about just over your head. Now, if you want to interfere with that natural process, just keep your head up. It's called the *boom*, and if anyone wants to know why it's called that, all they have to do is keep their head up!'

We all laughed nervously. He then asked for a volunteer to help him. Young Tom was the natural candidate. Thank goodness for 9-year-olds – I could have married him on the spot.

First of all, Bob and Tom slid the short side of the mainsail through a groove in the boom, which was lying on the deck. Then Bob pointed to the bottom of the mast, where we could see three pieces of rope poking out. He selected one of these, which he called the *mainsail halyard*, and attached it to the top corner of the mainsail. Then he pulled hard on this rope and, with Tom guiding one side of the sail through a groove that ran the length of the mast, the mainsail miraculously shot to the top. Bob fastened the loose end of this rope to the base of the mast, and finally, he and Tom attached the boom to a universal fitting on the mast.

'That's the mainsail up,' announced Bob. 'Now we have this little sail that goes on to the front. Does anyone know what it's called?'

There was an embarrassed silence as we all looked at each other furtively. Then Tom piped up: 'A jib!' We all looked at him gratefully.

The jib didn't have a mast to go up on; instead, it was hooked on to a wire (called the *forestay*) that ran from about two-thirds of the way up the mast down to the bow (the front of the boat). This time it was Sandy who, on Bob's instructions, attached the top corner of the jib to another of the pieces of rope at the bottom of the mast and hoisted the sail up the forestay. Again, the loose end of this rope – the *jib halyard* – was tightly caught at the base of the mast, next to the mainsail halyard.

Unlike the mainsail, the jib has to be directly controlled by a rope – the *jibsheet* – which is divided into two equal parts. The middle is attached to the loose corner of the jib, and the ends brought to either side of the boat and inserted into cleats on the top of each side. You *are* following this, aren't you?

As Bob inserted one end of the rope into the cleat nearest him, he said, 'Now, to stop the rope from slipping out of the cleat, we need a knot – your first!' He demonstrated a 'stopper' knot, which was a simple variation of

Knots

Sheet bend

Figure-of-eight ('stopper' knot)

Rolling hitch

Clove hitch

Bowline

Round turn & two half-hitches

Securing ropes to cleats

Make one complete turn around the cleat, before making two or three criss-cross turns over the 'horns'. If the rope is to be in position for some time, finish with a half-hitch.

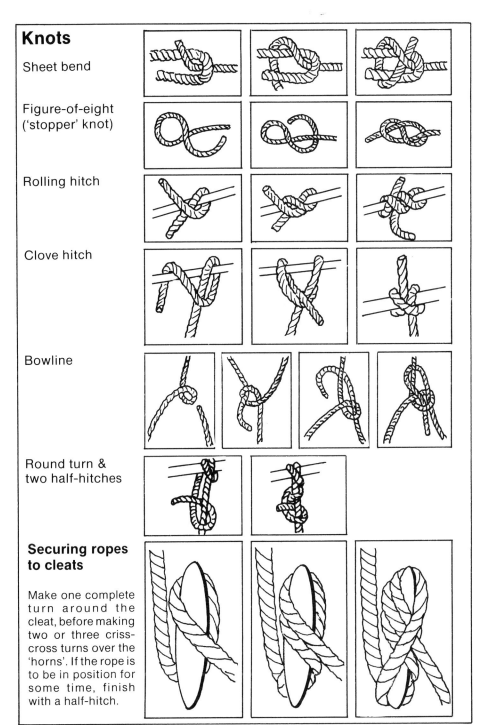

Day 2 continued

Day 2 continued

the common-or-garden type you use to tie your shoes. All right so far, Bob. I'd been dreading all the complicated ropework that seems to go with sailing, so I was relieved to find that, as the week progressed, we learned how to do all the required knots (*see p. 29*) as we went along. By the end of the course, they had become second nature.

Now that both the mainsail and the jib had been hoisted, Bob showed us how to stow the slack of the two halyards in neat, very shipshape coils that were hung from hooks at the side of the mast. He explained how important this was: if you needed to lower either sail quickly, it was no good if the ropes had got in a tangle – you need to be able to release them *instantly*.

Next we moved to the back end – the *stern* – of the boat, where Bob pointed out the rudder, which is responsible for the direction that the boat travels. This is pushed down when the boat is in deep enough water, but is raised up out of the way when nearing land, so that it doesn't break off. Bob showed us how to attach the tiller to the rudder: this stick would be our means of steering.

Opposite
Getting to grips with knots

The first person to sail around the world alone was a Canadian. Captain Joshua Slocum set out in 1895 in his 36-foot sloop *Spray*, completing the voyage three years later. He continued to sail single-handed until one day in 1909, when he and *Spray* left harbour never to be seen again.

While we were at this end of the boat, we dealt with the mainsheet, the rope that is attached to the tiller end of the mainsail as well as to the end of the boom. You control the boom – and, therefore, the mainsail that rises out of it – with the mainsheet.

Bob introduced Paul and the two other instructors who, with Bob, would be teaching us, and then he delivered his bombshell: each of us were going to be assigned to one of the four Wayfarers and then the instructors (one to each boat) would see how much of the rigging lecture we'd taken in. Bob's confidence in us was clearly greater than our own.

We were divided up into twos and threes, the instructors taking great care to separate all members of the same family. I couldn't understand why at first, but later, it was explained that they were

Day 2 continued

Day 2 continued

determined to have everyone start on an equal basis, with no previous relationships to hinder instruction. As a result, I was teamed up with Mike, while his son Tom was assigned to another Wayfarer with David and Sandy. When Tom found out, he was outraged – that's what I call a real fan! (Within five minutes, he'd forgotten all about us. Charming!)

Next we were directed to the sail loft, a large room containing dozens of sails, strung from pulleys. Mike and I collected a mainsail and a jib (after a lot of in-depth discussion as to what on earth they were), and then returned to our Wayfarer. To say we'd forgotten everything we'd been told would be the understatement of the year, but miraculously, bit by bit, with a lot of cheating and with encouragement from the instructors (who were loving every moment of it), Mike and I managed some semblance of Bob's rigging. Gradually, it all began to come together, and we finished with a real feeling of satisfaction.

We didn't have time to sit back and admire our handiwork – oh,

no, we now had to go straight on to the water. I was quite surprised. I think we'd all imagined that we wouldn't get into the Menai Strait until the last day or so, but this course primarily involved learning by practical experience. So when we found out that, even before lunch on our first day, we were going to be sailing, a wave of high spirits swept through the class.

First, though, we had to be dressed properly. We struggled into our wetsuits, boots and waterproofs – which not only repelled water but were also wonderfully windproof. The waterproofs came in two parts: a hooded jacket which you put on over the baggiest dungarees imaginable. Not quite the last word in fashion, but intended to slip over anything you might be wearing.

Getting into the water was itself quite a process. We all eagerly dragged our Wayfarers, loaded on their trolleys, down the slipway to the water's edge, but this wasn't as easy as it sounds. The boats were quite heavy and, unless you were careful, could build up quite a momentum all on their own. After I'd completely flattened Mike, Bob warned us not to try to steer them from the front: better to hold on at the back and sides, to slow them down if necessary.

Opposite
'Mike, are you sure it goes here?'

Day 2 continued

We had to roll the trolleys into the water so that the Wayfarers simply floated off. After Mike untied the rope that held our boat, I had to push the trolley back up the slipway. Then Bob, Mike and I clambered aboard.

We began by familiarizing ourselves with all the equipment on board and with which ropes controlled what. Bob showed us how the rudder had to be lifted so that it wouldn't drag on the bottom in shallow water. He also explained how to use the centre-board – a movable keel that is raised and lowered, depending on the direction of the boat and the depth of the water.

Sailing, said Bob, is all about reading the elements, and always knowing where the wind is coming from. Obviously, in a breeze, you can feel the wind on your face, and you can look out for the way flags or columns of smoke are blowing; the good old licked-finger-in-the-air method, while

Hoisting the mainsail

Day 2 continued

Day 2 continued

not high tech, is often as efficient as any. But did you know that seagulls always sit in the water with their beaks facing into the wind? As the week progressed, I found that I could read the wind by seeing which way my hair was blowing about.

Our first bit of real sailing was believe it or not, learning how to stop! Bob took us out a short way, and then let go of the tiller at the same time as he loosened the mainsail and the jib, so that both the sails flapped powerlessly. Now the Wayfarer seemed to have a mind of its own, gradually turning until it was at right angles to the wind, and bobbing up and down in the water, but making no headway.

'This,' said Bob, 'is the basic "hove-to" position. You'll be using it every time you want to stop: when you're mooring your boat, changing position with your crew and, especially, when you need to work out what you're doing wrong.'

Then, using the tiller again to turn the boat into the wind and pulling on the mainsheet so that the sail filled once more, he began what was to be the hallmark of the week's course: the continuous repetition of basic principles. Every manoeuvre in sailing has an inherent rhythm, and the Plas Menai instructors drummed in the order and routine of each one so that, by the end, all

> In 1933, an officer on the bridge of the USS *Ramapo*, then cruising in the South Pacific, was idly watching the ocean when, appalled, he caught sight of the crest of a wave that was in line with the horizon and the ship's crow's nest. Using these two coordinates, he was able – after the ship successfully scaled the wave – to establish that it had been 112 feet high, the tallest wave ever recorded in the open sea.

the basics were as familiar to us as breathing.

We spent the rest of the morning sailing *close-hauled* – that is, sailing as close as possible to the wind – and learning how to tack. This is a 90-degree turn produced while the boat is sailing towards the wind, and is used when you want to turn into the wind (*see diagram*). Everything was taken at a leisurely pace, primarily because there was very little wind. (Thank you, someone.)

First of all, Bob took the helm (i.e. he sat in the stern and operated the tiller and mainsheet) and demonstrated how to tack. By pushing the tiller hard away from him, telling Mike to loosen the jib so that it flapped, ducking while the boom swung over to the other side and then tightening both the mainsail and the jib, which were now billowing out on the other side of the mast, he

Day 2 continued

How to tack

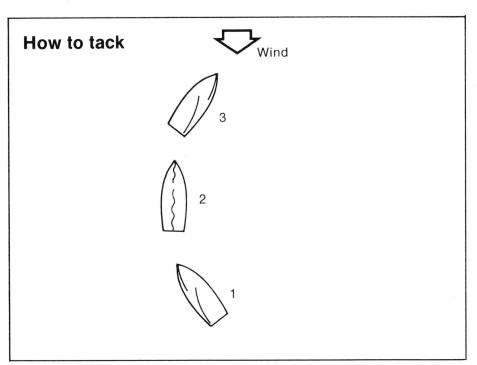

How to gybe

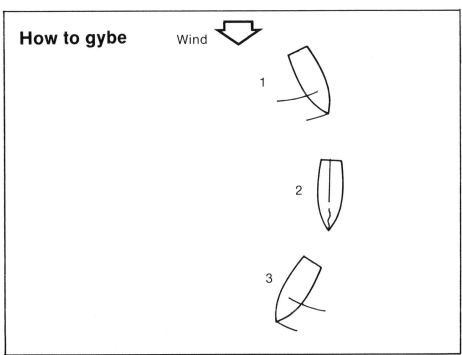

was able to change the direction of the boat in a matter of seconds. Bob tacked left and right a few times until we'd got the idea, and then he let us have a go.

I took the helm first, with Mike as crew and Bob as the fount of all wisdom. I sat at the edge of the boat, roughly in the middle, with Mike next to me, controlling the jib. I found that everything in sailing is done at right angles to the tiller. When it was time to tack, I looked around to check that we weren't heading for a buoy or boat or body, and then I said, 'Ready about.' This warned Mike of the impending tack so that he loosened the jib-sheet. Once he'd done this, he shouted 'Ready!' I then reversed the way I was holding the main-sheet and the tiller, so that the hand nearest the bow held the tiller and the one nearest the stern held the mainsheet.

Then the moment of greatest danger arrived – or so it seemed to me. I pushed the tiller away from me, to turn the boat, and warned Mike by saying, 'Lee oh.' As the boat turned, he and I crouched low and, while I still held on to the tiller and main-sheet, we moved across to the other side as the boom swung deliberately across in the other direction, just above our heads.

Everything seemed to happen in slow motion, with a time lapse between moving the tiller and the boom crossing over. When I looked up, I found that, while we remained more or less at the same place in the Strait, we were now sailing at about a 90-degree angle from where we'd started.

The mainsail was now flapping. Bob showed me how to pull on the mainsheet – holding on to it with the same hand as the tiller and hauling in more rope with the other – so that the sail became taut again. He then showed Mike how to pull on the jibsheet, to make sure that the jib didn't flap in the wind, and to fasten it tightly in the cleat on the side of the boat.

That first time, when every-thing worked, I felt terrific. Descriptions of sailing techniques are very difficult to understand – nothing seems to have any logic to it – but out there on the water, you can see instantly how every-thing works, and why.

When tacking, the boat is constantly turning round in the water, and you're moving from one side of the boat to the other; consequently, it's very easy to become disorientated. Bob ex-plained how, to get over this, we should pick out a point on each bank of the Strait and, depending on which direction we were going to turn, aim for one or the other. This was easy here; the banks were dotted with churches, houses and villages. But I did wonder how on earth anyone

Day 2 continued

could sail across the open sea, with nothing on the horizon to give a bearing.

During the next hour, I must have tacked across the Strait at least 20 times, and after a while, only the words 'Ready about', 'Ready' and 'Lee oh' broke the silence. I just carried on doing the same thing, again and again and again, until I was sure that I could perform that manoeuvre

The film crew. I'm sure they didn't plan on making it harder for me to learn to sail!

in my sleep, and, like riding a bicycle, I would never forget how.

We returned to Plas Menai and, mooring the boat to a buoy near the slipway, Bob announced that we had to put the Wayfarer into 'lunchtime position'. We hauled down the mainsail, wrapping it round the boom as we went. When this was done, we pulled the boom off the mast and stowed it in the hull, the mainsheet remaining attached to the tiller. Then we wrapped the jib neatly around the forestay, re-

The problems of filming

Day 2 continued

attaching it to the shackle in the middle of the jibsheet.

Our return to the shore was heralded by hysterical barking from Trevor, who'd abandoned his hiding place and was in a state of apoplexy. He swam out to meet us, tail wagging like a propeller, and escorted us back to the slipway in high excitement.

'Er, Bob – meet Trevor,' I said in answer to the look of amazement on his face. I hurriedly added, 'He's our mascot, and I'm so sorry we brought him along, but you won't hear from him

Mike at the helm

Day 2 continued

again, I promise.'

Since the rule about dogs not being allowed at the Centre is so strict, we all reckoned that Bob took the news of Trevor's arrival like a man and will win a medal from the RSPCA. Particularly since Trevor rather appreciatively showered him with half the Menai Strait in a spontaneous burst of *bonhomie* . . .

We joined the film crew and the rest of the class for a celebratory lunch, relaxing near the sail loft and all swopping experiences. It was then I discovered that, apart from all our efforts out on the Strait, the film crew had had a whole set of problems of their own.

Because our Wayfarer was too small to take more than four people at any one time, they'd spent all morning thinking of ingenious ways of keeping as close as possible to us without actually being in the boat. I've got to hand it to them, they tried just about everything: shooting from a large, stationary wooden boat as we sailed past them, from a noisy speedboat alongside us and from a larger cruiser, finally being towed behind us in a little rowing boat.

The trouble was that Bob was determined that the filming should not get in the way of his sailing lesson. Just as the film crew would manoeuvre into position to get a great shot of us,

he'd flip the boat round to show us a new technique, and we'd be a vague speck on the horizon within minutes, leaving Digby the cameraman tearing his moustache out! There's only so much a zoom lens can do.

Lunch over, now it was Mike's turn to take the helm. We very quickly discovered that he had an oversteering problem: he'd push the tiller too far away from him and swing the boat too far round, perfecting a 360-degree turn. This was fine as long as you wanted to go all the way round, but a bit confusing if you just wanted to change direction! Each time, Mike assured us that he did, in fact, want to turn a complete circle – so he got 10 out of 10 for positive thinking.

Despite its rough-and-ready image, sailing is really quite a graceful sport, in which all manoeuvres have to be slow and deliberate and you have to be very sensitive to the movement of the boat and the direction and strength of the wind, tide and current. It took some time before Mike caught on to this – at first, he tackled every manoeuvre with the finesse of a Sumo wrestler – but finally he came to see that the boat would do as he wished as long as he was gentle and took his time.

While Mike was being put through his paces, I was glad to have the opportunity to look

Day 2 continued

around, not only to watch for any water-borne dangers but also to admire the wonderful scenery. (Mike's circles were an advantage – sweet of him to think of me!) The current was strong here and, as a consequence, we'd drifted quite a distance south-west, down the Strait. Soon the afternoon's sailing was rewarded with a glorious view of the massive walls of Caernarfon Castle. The tide was now on the turn, and as a result, some unfortunate sailors were sitting disconsolately in their

boat that had become stranded on a sandbank.

Bob took the helm and sailed Mike and me back to the Centre. So far, we'd been tacking into the wind, which had been taking us down the Strait out towards the Irish Sea. To get back to Plas Menai, Bob let out the sails fully to catch all the wind: this is called 'running with the wind' and, with the centreboard pulled right up, it made for a smooth, quick ride.

It was ideal yachting weather for beginners. The sea was calm, the sun was shining out of the bluest sky and there was just the faintest breeze – it was a perfect day. What was it that Rat said to Mole? 'There is *nothing* – absolutely nothing – half so much worth doing as simply messing about in boats.' Mike and I were bursting with *joie de vivre* – I can't describe the completeness you feel as you splash through the

Caernarfon Castle

In 1283, the English king, Edward I, having finally put down a Welsh revolt, began the construction of what would become Caernarfon Castle. During the building, he based himself and his queen, Eleanor of Castile, in a temporary wooden structure on the site. It was there, on 25 April 1284, that their first son, the unfortunate future Edward II, was born. When the boy was 17, the king revived the title of Prince of Wales, and conferred it on his son. (This had been unused since the year before the young Edward's birth, when the king had hanged, drawn and quartered the water, brushed by the spray, a tiny boat playing with the elements. However, as we neared Plas Menai, we reached a point in our training that we couldn't put off any longer, a procedure that changed my life overnight – the capsize drill.

As we were to find out in the days to come, capsizing is simply a fact of life to people who mess about in boats, and it was imperative that we learn how to overcome this emergency safely and quickly. I must admit, though, that it was terribly painful to capsize our Wayfarer *deliberately* after we'd just spent hours learning to keep upright and make everything work.

The three of us moved to one side of the boat and leaned over. The boat leaned over, too, and suddenly we were all in the water and the Wayfarer's mast was dipping in and out of the waves. Righting it was Mike's and my

responsibility; Bob was simply there to give us friendly advice.

As Mike and I bobbed up and down in the water, held up on the surface by our buoyancy aids, Bob told us that the most important thing to do in the event of a capsize is to *stay with the boat*. Unless it is holed, a boat will not sink, and it can then perform two functions: you can hang on to it to keep afloat, and it is much easier for rescuers to spot than a head in the water.

Under Bob's direction, Mike and I moved to the stern, where I checked that the rudder was secure. Mike then swam into the inside of the boat, found the mainsheet and handed the end to me, to use as a lifeline. I then made my way round the bottom of the boat to the centreboard, which was sticking out to the side. Mike found the jibsheet and threw it up over the side of the boat, hitting me smack in the

last Welsh prince, David ap Gruffydd.) Since that time, the English monarch's eldest son has always been made Prince of Wales.

Caernarfon is located at the south-western end of the Menai Strait and, with the castle at Beaumarais at the north-eastern end, efficiently sealed this vital waterway, the gateway to the grain

treasury that was the island of Anglesey. Caernarfon is extremely well defended itself, surrounded on 3½ sides by water: to the south by the River Seiont, to the west by the Menai Strait, and to the north and north-east by the tidal inlet of the River Cadnant.

Work on the castle was finally halted in 1330, before the interior

Day 2 continued

face! Despite this, I managed to reach up and hold on to the centreboard, at the same time pulling on the jibsheet. Meanwhile, Mike floated inside the boat, above the side now in the water; this way, he would be in the correct position to be inside the boat when it was righted, so that could help Bob and me to get back on board.

That, at least, was the theory; the reality was a little different. I clambered up on top of the centreboard and balanced myself so that I could stand upright.

Capsize!

Day 2 continued

(And now for my next trick . . .) Grasping the mainsheet in my two hands I tugged with all my strength, putting my weight behind it, so that the Wayfarer would swing back up. Nothing seemed to happen. Bob was just on the point of telling us that the worst thing that can happen after a capsize is for the boat to go *right* over, with the mast pointing down to the bottom of the sea – when the boat went right over, with the mast pointing down to the bottom of the sea. Afterwards, Bob told me that I should

Day 2 continued

have jumped up on the centre-board sooner, but for now, we had a perfectly inverted boat.

Luckily, Mike had obeyed Bob's urgent call to get out, and had swum away from the Wayfarer before it turned over, its sails now streaming upside down in the current. For some reason, I found our situation hysterically funny. I was crying with laughter as Mike and I climbed on to the edge of the underside of the boat and applied leverage to swing the mast up out of the water. Finally, it floated up until, at last, it was

Day 2 continued

parallel with the waves. Back to square one.

As Mike made his way round to the other side of the boat to take up his position again, Bob said: 'You know, pulling a boat out of the water is terribly easy – at least, it is nine times out of ten. However, here we have a major problem: you, Anneka!'

By this stage, I was laughing uncontrollably and soon everyone else was, too. If Mike and I hadn't been wearing our buoyancy aids, we would have drowned from our hysterics. But we had work to do, so in between guffaws, I tried to right the boat. Standing on the centreboard, I pulled and pulled and . . . pulled so hard that I overbalanced, fell off and had to start all over again.

The film crew was having an

Day 2 continued

equally hard time – trying to keep the camera still enough to film while everyone shook with laughter. To top it all, Bob kept calling out cheerfully, 'Hey, watch out for those jellyfish!'

When you're up on a slippery centreboard, about two feet above the water, pulling hard on a slender piece of rope and looking over the side of a boat at what seems like miles of mast and waterlogged sail to yank up, it can all seem an impossible task. However, on my third attempt, with a lot of encouragement from Bob and a growing feeling of responsibility for poor Mike stuck round the other side of the boat just waiting in the water, I found that the mast was beginning to yield to my weight. It finally rose majestically and the boat came upright, carrying Mike, inside the hull, with it. The film crew clapped and whistled their congratulations.

The Wayfarer was obviously now full of water, so after Bob and I clambered in, we all began bailing with a vengeance. Somehow the three of us ended up on the same side of the boat – or else all the water slopped over to one side – and, you've guessed it, we capsized again! By this stage, the drill was taking on all the features of a *Carry On* movie – and it was supposed to be something so easy that a 10-year-old could do it blindfolded.

Getting the boat upright wasn't so difficult this time – all that practice, you understand – and we were extra careful to keep to both sides of the boat as Mike and Bob bailed out the foot or so of water that sloshed around our feet. My job was to steer while the others bailed, but I was still laughing so much that I muddled up my ropes, and as we ran with the wind . . . I hate to have to say this, but, yes, we capsized for the

was completed. It has a long, irregular shape topped by polygonal towers; the biggest, the Eagle Tower, is on the west side, facing the Strait. Bands of different coloured limestone, some possibly from nearby, form decorative patterns on the walls. In fact, as castles go, this one is quite ornamental, but the decoration was not done at the expense of its fortifications, which were strong enough to repel the Welsh leader Owain Glyndwr in 1401 and 1403/4.

The castle was not, however, completely impregnable; its formidable defences eventually caused its downfall. In 1646, having become the focus of the Royalist cause in that part of the world, it came under

Day 2 continued

third time – or was it the fourth or fifth!

By now, Mike and I were simply helpless – both from our hysterics and from the sheer hard work. We were also frozen through: we'd been in the water now for about an hour, and my hands were totally white, cold and numb. In the end, we made a very undignified exit; the rescue boat, which had been shadowing us the whole time, came alongside and we fell in, and Bob sailed the Wayfarer home on his own.

Sorry, Bob!

By the time we got back, frizzled by the sun, frozen by the water, battered by the elements and exhausted, dinner was already in progress and there was only half an hour before the start of that night's lecture. I went straight to my room, stripped off my wet things and stood under the hot shower for 20 minutes, trying to warm myself through. I felt badly in need of emergency massage, balm for my sore face and lips and something for my

We never did get the boat the right way up

50

Day 2 continued

Day 2 continued

poor battered and bruised limbs. How fitting that the lecture was to be on safety and first aid . . .

Before going to the lecture room, I took all my damp clothing to hang up in the Centre's drying room, so it would be ready for tomorrow. As I opened the door, though, a stench of old socks and drying rubber sent me reeling back. I closed the door in shock and decided that putting on damp clothes in the morning was part of the fun.

The lecture rooms at Plas Menai are quite impressive, equipped with videos, screens and projectors. All 30 or so beginners sat on the chairs scattered around the room and chatted while we waited for Barry, who was to be our lecturer that night.

Because we'd had to do our capsize drill on our own to suit the requirements of the film crew, Mike and I were curious to find out how the rest of our class had fared. You can imagine our surprise when we discovered that they'd all had a whale of a time! The way the instructors at Plas Menai normally organize this part of the course is a lot of fun: everyone learns from each other's mistakes as they take it in turns to right a capsized Wayfarer, to the accompaniment of alternate barracking and encouragement from the rest of the class. None of them seemed to have had any particular difficulty learning to right the boat, so Mike and I just kept quiet . . .

All talk stopped as Barry came round the table at the front of the room and asked, 'What do you think is the single most dangerous thing that could happen when you're sailing?'

'Storms' and 'Rocks' were some of the suggestions proffered by the class – 'Being on a boat with Anneka' came from Mike. 'Of

siege from the Roundheads, finally surrendering in June. After the Restoration in 1660, Charles II ordered it to be pulled down but, luckily, his command seems to have been ignored.

Although all the eldest sons of the English monarchs from the time of Edward I had been Princes of Wales, the first to receive that title in Wales itself was the future Edward VIII. Due to the influence of Lloyd George, MP for the area, Caernarfon Castle was chosen as the site of the investiture. The next time the castle received this singular honour was in 1969, when the Prince of Wales took part in a ceremony devised by the Earl of Snowdon.

course, these things are really dangerous,' Barry agreed, 'but the number one danger when you're sailing is *hypothermia* – that is, a very low body temperature, which some of you may know as "exposure"' (*see below*). As Barry outlined the symptoms, I realized how close Mike and I had come to being prime exhibits at his lecture.

'You are vulnerable to hypothermia at *all* times,' he continued, 'and you must watch out for the symptoms in yourself and in your crew. No matter how experienced you are, you are always susceptible to this condition, which literally creeps up on you.

'The most alarming thing about hypothermia is that it makes you more and more careless. For example, if you were making your way back to port and it was later than you'd planned and you were all tired, cold and suffering from the effects of all that wind, you'd

probably not take the time to wrap up a bit more warmly; you'd just carry on beating against the wind. You'd begin to make the wrong decisions as your brain started to slow down. At the least, you might just sit in a little huddle on your own, not realizing that you were gradually closing down; at the worst, if the sea was a bit rough, you and your crew might end up capsizing, with potentially disastrous consequences.' (Mike and I stole furtive glances at each other at this point.)

Barry reached under the table and brought out what looked like a very bad example of extreme hypothermia: an armless and legless torso topped by a bald head. 'This,' said Barry, 'is Ethel. She's very good, never complains,' and he unceremoniously dumped her on to the table with a thud. 'Ethel' was actually a dummy with an obligingly expanding

Hypothermia

It can get very cold on the surface of the water, and if you happen to spend time in it, becoming chilled is almost a certainty. For most people, this will show itself by shivers and shakes, but sometimes the cold will penetrate beyond the surface skin, into the vital organs at the core of the body. If the 'core temperature' goes down beyond a certain point, the person will be suffering from *hypothermia* and his life is in danger.

How can you tell if someone is suffering from hypothermia? He will stop shivering, his movements will become very sluggish and he solar plexus, designed to be used to demonstrate emergency resuscitation – the 'kiss of life' (*instructions are on p. 56*). As Barry tilted Ethel's head back to open the airway, pinched her nostrils and blew into her mouth, it was uncanny how lifelike she seemed as her chest rose and fell.

Dropping Ethel casually under the table again, Barry asked us to suggest what sorts of emergency gear we should take with us when we went out sailing. 'Flares,' said someone, 'A bottle of brandy,' said another ('Oh, no,' said Barry), and 'A first aid kit.' The things that nobody in the class thought of were paddles (if there is absolutely no wind or the mast comes down), a bucket (for bailing), a proper anchor that is firmly attached to the boat with a rope, a whistle, distress flags and a towline. Barry then demonstrated the 'Help!' wave – when you stand in the boat and move both arms up and down at your sides – which is used only in emergency situations so that there is no doubt that this is *not* just a friendly wave but that help is needed.

Barry explained how important it was to check that everything in and on the boat was seaworthy before setting out, and to tell a responsible person when you're going out and when you're due back. 'Don't forget to tell them when you *do* get back,' he added, 'You won't make any friends if you turn up after a rescue party has been sent out to look for you!'

Because we'd missed dinner, Mike, the film crew and I went to nearby Port Dinorwic for a quick bite to eat and a post-mortem of the day's progress. I couldn't get over how lucky I'd been to be teamed up with Mike. His sense of humour had had me laughing all day (although this had proved deadly during the capsize drill),

may become mentally confused. His skin will be pale and may take on a bluish tinge. He may lose consciousness, his breathing may become shallow and his pulse weak, and if his temperature isn't raised, he may die.

What can you do to help? First, prevent any further heat loss – e.g. get the person out of the water as quickly as possible and provide what shelter you can in the circumstances. Wrap him in blankets (a shiny 'space blanket' is ideal), or use your own body heat to warm him. If he is still conscious, give him a warm (*not* hot), sweet drink. If the casualty is relatively young, you could place him in a warm bath. Do not, however, do this with

Day 2 continued

The all-important safety
lectures

an elderly person – the shock may be fatal. Finally, you should summon medical help as soon as possible.

Never give alcohol. *Never* wrap an electric blanket around a casualty or give him a hot water bottle: this will cause blood to rush to the skin surface, away from vital organs.

Sir Francis Chichester, who went round the world in *Gypsy Moth IV*, in 1966–67 when he was in his mid sixties, had earlier been interested in flying. In 1929 he took a course of instruction and in 1936 made several pioneer flights, the first being a solo to Australia.

Day 2 continued

Artificial resuscitation

On all sailing courses, you will be constantly supervised by instructors who are fully qualified in first aid techniques. However, once you have learned enough to go out on the water unsupervised, and especially if you are planning to buy your own boat, you must be trained in the basic resuscitation methods. The following gives instructions for artificial resuscitation – the 'kiss of life' – but the very best way of learning this (and heart compression, which is the next technique to try if a person's heart stops beating) is to take one of the first aid courses offered by both St John's Ambulance and the British Red Cross.

If casualty is not breathing, place one hand under his neck and press down on his forehead with the other. This will open airway.

Keep neck arched. Hold chin forward with one hand. Pinch nostrils closed with fingers of the other.

Take a deep breath. Seal casualty's mouth with yours. Blow two good breaths into his mouth. Check that chest is rising and falling.

Check casualty's pulse. If heart is beating, continue to give breaths every five seconds until casualty starts to breathe on his own.

Once breathing has commenced, place casualty in recovery position and summon medical help.

and was a good foil to my lack of patience. For example, when we were doing the rigging, we'd had to take the mainsail all the way down after doing something wrong, but while I'd kicked the boat and moaned, Mike had simply got on with it. On the sea, we were like a comedy act – in between laughing, we were in a state of chaos. I'd ask, 'Do you feel happy, Mike?' and he'd reply, 'No, just fear!'

He was a very gentle man, especially with Tom, and very encouraging with me. He would say, 'You're doing a grand job, Annie. You've cracked it, you've cracked it!' as I steered into the wind with sails flapping, careered all over the place and capsized. 'You've cracked it, Annie, that's exactly right!'

His words echoed in my mind as I made my way upstairs. Collapsing with total exhaustion on to the bed, I only had time to remember that I *had* been quite good at tacking, before I fell deeply asleep.

DAY 3

I lay in bed in a half-conscious state, wondering why I could hear rain and wind. There was a good reason for this: I staggered to the window and pulled back the curtains to see steady rain and a howling wind – an *urgent*, bellowing wind that threw itself against the window pane. The sea was cloaked in a thick, grey cloud.

Oh well, I thought, *they won't get us sailing in* that *today*.

Not so! The Centre was up for business as usual. Although it was a ghastly, disgusting day from a filming point of view, it was an ordinary sailing day as far as those at Plas Menai were concerned. Somehow, sailing makes you incredibly intrepid; it's as if you know what you're letting yourself in for when you take up

a sport like this – you *expect* Force 8 gales and lashing rain. So I suppose that I wasn't surprised when Bob and the rest of the instructors seemed totally undeterred by the depressing scene outside. Anyway, if you operate an outdoor sports school in Britain, you really can't wait for the sun.

As Mike and I made our way down to our Wayfarer, we found the film crew standing round the boat getting ready to fix a camera to the top of the mast. A small crowd had gathered.

'Just watch this,' I said to Mike, bursting with professional pride. 'Digby, our cameraman, is going to shin up the mast to secure the camera in place – what an athlete! This man will stop at nothing!'

As I turned back to watch this

In 1976, while sailing from Florida to Britain to take part in the *Observer* Singlehanded Transatlantic Race, the American Philip Weld and the crew of the 60-foot trimaran *Gulf Streamer* found themselves faced with a 40-foot, double-crested wave. It overturned them, leaving them stranded 350 miles from the US coast. However, they were prepared for such an emergency: entering the access hole that had been cut into the bottom of the main (centre) hull, they lived in the boat for five days until a passing ship, seeing their distress flares, came to their rescue.

heroic display, the lads tipped the boat over on its side, casually bent over and fixed the camera on to the mast, now lying on the ground.

'I'd have never believed it unless I'd seen it with my own eyes,' said Mike. 'I'm impressed.'

He and I rigged the boat (not a bad second attempt), but before we could get on to the water, Paul gathered us together in the sail room for an impromptu lecture on the 'Points of Sailing'. The rain was getting quite serious by now, so it was a good delaying tactic and filled the time nicely.

Using a large blackboard, Paul showed us the whole range of sailing manoeuvres you can make in relation to the wind (*see diagram*). We'd all learned yesterday about sailing close to the wind ('close-hauled') when we tacked, and how to avoid sailing too close to the wind in the 'no-go' zone. That had been quite straight-forward: we'd found that you could sail very close to the wind if the sails were tightly pulled in, but the moment you overstepped the mark and got too close, the jib would start flapping – the warning sign to bear away a little. Then we'd learned how to sail at right angles to the wind, with the sails let out about half-way, cupping in the wind – called being on a 'beam reach'.

Now Paul showed us that, if we were to bear away even more,

we'd be on a 'broad reach', with the wind nearly behind us. By bearing away still more, and with the centreboard fully raised, we'd be 'running', the boat almost gliding along with the sails as fully out as possible to catch the wind that was now directly at our backs. To turn either left or right while we were running, we'd either have to turn towards the wind again ('luffing') or gybe – and we'd be learning how to do that next.

Lecture over, Mike and I joined Bob down at the quayside. As the wind whipped around us, Mike looked worried. Not about us – no, he was concerned about how Tom would manage in these con-ditions. Bob said that the weather was 'gusty and boisterous' (I would have described it as lethal), and he made sure that we had all our safety equipment secured properly.

This was a good moment to run through everything Barry had lectured us about the pre-vious evening. With the wind really getting up, we had a lurking suspicion that the weather might have a capsize in store for us, so we took great care to make sure that we were as fully equipped

Opposite
Digby, the cameraman

58

Day 3 continued

Points of sailing

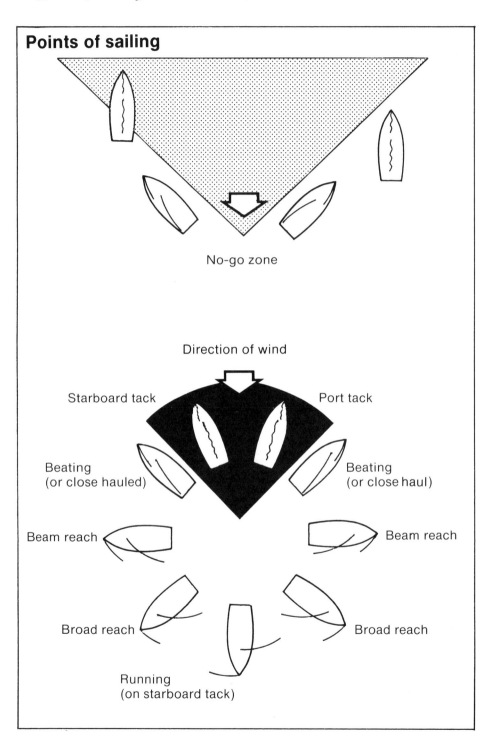

No-go zone

Direction of wind

Starboard tack   Port tack

Beating
(or close hauled)   Beating
(or close haul)

Beam reach   Beam reach

Broad reach   Broad reach

Running
(on starboard tack)

safety-wise as possible. As well as the requisite paddles, bailing bucket and anchor, I wondered if we shouldn't take along some flares as well, but Bob said that we were never going to sail out of sight of the Centre, and even then we'd be continually accompanied by the rescue boats.

The last thing we had to check, under Bob's supervision, was the boat's buoyancy: ensuring that there wasn't any water slopping around in the hull. Bob pointed out some cat-door-like flaps on either side of the bottom, called 'self-bailers', which we had to make sure were shut. Then we had to go to the back – sorry, *stern* – of the Wayfarer, unscrew the drain plug, or 'bung', and rock the boat as far to one side as possible to let any water drain out. Usually only a pint or two

Getting ready to go

Day 3 continued

comes out, but obviously, if there's a lot, you should suspect a crack in the hull.

Finally, all safety checks done, we were allowed on the boat. I still find it baffling why we enjoyed going out on the water in all that wild weather. Sailing definitely does something to you. If I were back in London, I'd be constantly diving for cover between taxis and the warm indoors. Yet here we were – unbelievably – full of idiotic glee at the prospect of battling the elements again. And this was *real* sailing, unlike the day before when we'd spent our time simply pottering about, lucky to get any wind at all.

With Bob on board to watch out for such dangers as collisions with other Wayfarers and stray windsurfers, we felt quite safe. He had a very reassuring manner, managing to keep his voice quite calm and steady each time either Mike or I made a false move that sent the boat heeling over rather alarmingly or the boom swinging in an unexpected direction. He kept coaching us soothingly, coaxing the sailors out of us, telling us to feel for the little changes in the wind's direction, making *us* tell *him* what we thought we were doing wrong and encouraging us when things went smoothly. Well, not exactly smoothly, but at least according to plan.

We quickly learned that, apart from flat, calm, windless days, there was no such thing as smooth sailing. It's all pretty exciting stuff. When you're at the helm, with your hands on the tiller and mainsheet, it's like controlling an out-of-control coach-and-four round an obstacle course – and we all know what that feels like!

First, Bob checked that we remembered how to tack, but after all the repetitive training of yesterday, I don't think I could have forgotten if I'd tried. Then he took us through the points of sailing into the wind (the boat heeled over worryingly), and then running with the wind, when we zipped along smooth and fast.

We hadn't been sailing for very long when Bob told us to head for shore – easily frightened, these experienced sailors . . . Actually, I have to admit that we were quite relieved when Bob made that decision. Mike and I had been determined not to be the first in the class to chicken out, but buffeted as we were by the blustery wind, there definitely seemed to be something like wild seahorses tugging the boat in every direction. I think everyone in our class had been hanging on for grim death for the same foolhardy reason: the moment we turned into a little sheltered cove called Cable Bay, the rest followed suit.

As we neared the shore, we turned into the wind and let go of all the ropes, so that the sails flapped and the boats stopped. Making sure that the rudders and centreboards were raised, we hauled our Wayfarers a little way up the pebbly shore. One person from each boat had to hold on to the forestay (the wire to which the jib is attached), while someone else selected a large rock to which they secured the 'painter'; this is the piece of rope attached to the bottom of the mast which you use to tie up your boat. With the wind the way it was that day, Bob and Paul told us to keep a close eye on our Wayfarers at all times because securing them like this wasn't all that safe.

Then we all had to lower our mainsails, wrap them round the booms, detach the booms from

Learning to reef

Day 3 continued

the masts and place them in the bottom of the boats. Gathering on the shore, we gratefully hugged beakers of steaming coffee that Paul had poured from huge thermos flasks, while we learned all about reefing.

Bob explained that it was too gusty to cope with a full amount of sail and still learn anything, so we had to make the mainsail smaller – in other words, we had to *reef* it. That way, we wouldn't go so fast and the boat would be more manageable. To make the sail smaller, we simply had to roll the bottom of it several times around the boom, like a roller

Coffee break

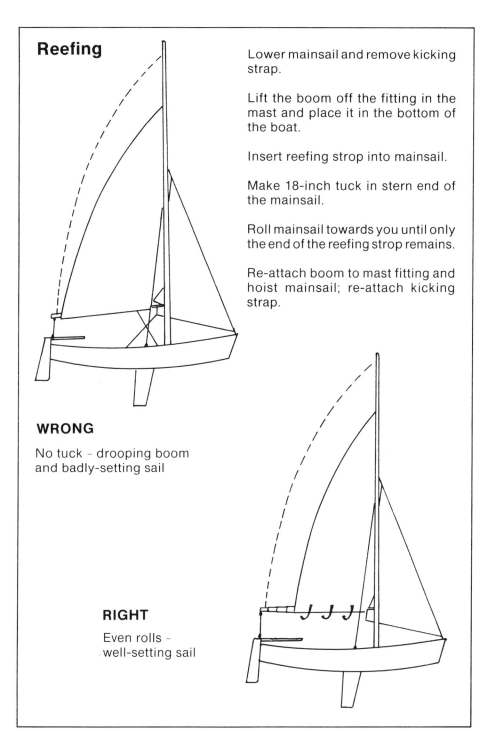

Reefing

Lower mainsail and remove kicking strap.

Lift the boom off the fitting in the mast and place it in the bottom of the boat.

Insert reefing strop into mainsail.

Make 18-inch tuck in stern end of the mainsail.

Roll mainsail towards you until only the end of the reefing strop remains.

Re-attach boom to mast fitting and hoist mainsail; re-attach kicking strap.

WRONG

No tuck - drooping boom and badly-setting sail

RIGHT

Even rolls - well-setting sail

blind, so that its top corner didn't reach right to the top of the mast. Bob reckoned that we had to reduce the height of the sail by about three feet – roughly three times round the boom. Conference finished, we returned to our boats.

While Mike held the Wayfarer fast by the forestay and turned it into the wind (why does he always get the easy jobs?), I reefed as Bob shouted instructions. I took the boom from the bottom of the boat where we'd stowed it, placed it across my lap and unwrapped the loosely bundled mainsail. Then Bob handed me a length of blue rope with a loop at one end. He explained that, once I'd wound part of the mainsail around the boom, the fitting for the kicking strap (the rope that leads from the boom to the bottom of the boat, to prevent the boom from rising) would be rolled up, too. If we wound the blue rope – technically called the *reefing strop* – inside the sail, the looped end that remained outside could act as the kicking strap fitting.

It was a bit of a fiddle tucking in the blind end of the reefing strop while trying to roll the mainsail as tightly as possible round the boom – and Mike wasn't a great deal of help, just standing there in the water holding the boat and laughing. I also had to make a tuck in the first roll to keep the mainsail as straight as possible. Eventually, though, after a bit of a struggle, I had the boom neatly swaddled in the mainsail and back in the mast.

The finishing touch was to hoist the mainsail into position by yanking hard on the halyard, and then secure that rope by winding it in a 'figure of eight' around a double cleat at the base of the mast. Feeling incredibly domesticated (and, besides, I was being filmed at the time), I neatly coiled the slack and hung this on the upper cleat.

The reefed mainsail was now about three feet short of the top of the mast. Miraculously, the reefing strop held firm as I attached the kicking strap to it. We all climbed back into our boats, sailed out of the cove . . . and it worked! With less sail to control, we had much less of a fight on our hands, and the boats were much easier to handle.

Since it was nearly lunchtime, we headed back to Plas Menai and, because the weather was so foul, decided to have lunch at the Centre rather than eat our soggy sandwiches in the dripping rain. The thought of taking off our very wet wetsuits and getting dry, only to have to put on the damp wetsuits again, was too much for the three of us. So, we sat down to eat still dressed for the weather outside.

Back on the Wayfarer, Mike

Day 3 continued

Day 3 continued

now took the helm and we tried to consolidate everything we'd learned so far. However, the weather conspired to give us a thoroughly frustrating afternoon: we'd be doing fine, Bob would remark on how much more stable the boat was, and just as he finished speaking, a freak gust of wind would almost send us over.

Witnesses to all this were the film crew, sailing near us in another Wayfarer so that they could do some tracking shots. Yesterday, we'd found it very difficult to communicate over the relatively huge area of the Strait. When the film crew was waiting patiently for us, we always seemed to be heading off in the opposite direction. When Mike, Bob and I were ready, they were busy with something else. Today, however, each boat was supplied with a walkie-talkie – ours was in our bailing bucket! – so that we could keep up a two-way dialogue.

This was not without its grimly funny moments. For instance, we'd be in the middle of a very difficult manoeuvre, hanging on for dear life, speeding over the waves at 8 knots, nearly capsizing – when our director's voice would crackle into the bucket: 'Come towards us on a beam reach, put a tack in and sail away from us in a north-north-westerly direction.' Yeah, yeah, yeah, and why don't we try some break-dancing at the same time? Poor Mike! Having to be Francis Chichester and a film star all at the same time!

He and I changed over again. As I struggled to keep the boat on an even keel, Bob told us calmly to look over our shoulders and observe one of the basic rules of navigation: 'At sea, power should give way to sail, but not always . . .'

Mike and I looked over our shoulders and then quickly back at Bob, aghast. Bearing down on us out of nowhere was an enormous tanker! OK, I got the idea, and without having to check with Bob, I swung the Wayfarer into a determined tack, sailing away as fast as I could.

Although our encounter with the tanker had been a bit alarming, I don't think we were ever in any real danger. Especially judging by the way Bob waved to the tanker's bridge and the reciprocal horn blasts we were honoured with in reply.

I thought that was enough messing about with boats for one day, but no, Bob decided it was time to teach us how to gybe.

Instead of sailing at an angle *towards* the wind, Bob turned the Wayfarer *away* from it, so that the wind was pushing us along

Opposite
The film crew at work

Day 3 continued

from behind and we were 'running'. To capture the maximum amount of wind power, the sails were let out as far as they'd go without flapping, and with the centreboard fully up, we skimmed along the surface, a bit like windsurfers.

Now came the tricky bit . . . After checking that we weren't in for any collisions, Bob warned his crew (me this time) by calling, 'Stand by to gybe!' Then he moved towards the middle of the boat and gently pushed the tiller towards where he had been sitting until the boom looked as if it wanted to swing the other way.

By now, I'd released the jib so that too was flapping.

Bob warned Mike and me that, any second now, the boom was going to come thundering across to the other side of the boat so that wind could fill the opposite side of the mainsail. Keen to save our skulls, we crouched down. At this point, Bob was watching the boom so that, as it started to swing, he could warn us by calling out, 'Gybe oh!' As it whizzed over our heads, he straightened the tiller and then sat down on the opposite side of the boat while I pulled in the jib, fixing the jibsheet loosely through the cleat,

Opposite
Preparing for stormy weather

'Where did that come from?'

Day 3 continued

so that this sail gathered in as much wind as possible. The gybe now complete, both sails were bulging with wind at exactly the same angle as they had been before, but now on the other side of the boat.

It hadn't been so bad after all. After Mike and I experimented taking the helm and gybing a bit, we found that the main difference between tacking and gybing was that we really had to wait for the right moment to gybe. We had to turn the boat more and more in the direction we wanted to go, almost teasing the sails; then they reached a point where they couldn't take any more wind on that side, and that was when the boom just *had* to swing back the other way. It was all very logical; it just took a little sensitivity.

Bob wanted to take us through a few more gybes, but conditions soon became just too dangerous to do any more. This also meant that we wouldn't be going solo as planned – 'solo' in the sense that Mike and I would be on our own in the boat, while Bob, in one of the rescue boats, would watch, advise and probably wince.

Although we were disappointed, under the circumstances we wouldn't have wanted it any other way. By the end of that afternoon, when I took over the helm for the final time, I simply couldn't understand why I was doing everything wrong. Then Bob took over, and to my relief, even he had trouble keeping the boat going at a steady pace because of the freak gusts. Finally, there was nothing for it but to return to Plas Menai, wet, cold and completely exhausted.

In his bright red and yellow jacket and woolly hat, Tom gave us an ecstatic welcome as we came ashore, a bright speck in all that gloom. He was full of the news of how his boat had cap-

The word *yacht* has come to be synonymous with the luxury cruising boats much frequented by the international jet set. However, according to the *Oxford English Dictionary*, a 'yacht' is a 'light sailing-vessel kept, and usually specially built and rigged, for racing' or 'a vessel propelled by sails, steam, electricity, or motive power other than oars, and used for private pleasure excursions, cruising, travel, etc.' In other words, a yacht can be anything from the smallest dinghy to the largest sea-going racer.

Day 3 continued

sized. 'It was horrible,' he said. 'The boat went right over!'

'Oh well,' I said, trying to salvage at least one silver lining from all the clouds in the sky, 'having sailed in this, you're ready to sail around the world . . .'

It was only then I realized that, throughout all this, we'd been accompanied by a tirade of barking. Trevor? Oh, no, please not Trevor! We thought we'd tucked him safely out of harm's – and Bob's – way.

'He's kept that up all afternoon,' said Tom brightly.

One glance at Bob's face, and Ray and I raced up the slipway to salvage the situation. Apparently, Trevor had serenaded the entire Centre all afternoon – his 'kennel' acting as a natural amphitheatre and projecting his high spirits into all the lecture rooms and offices. Sorry, Bob . . .

I was soon leaning against the wall of my shower, letting the hot water and steam gradually bring me back to life. I luxuriated in the thought of an hour's peace before supper at 7.00 *sharp*. And then came a nervous little tap on my bedroom door . . .

How did our director put it? 'First the good news. You can go to bed now and have a sleep. Now the bad news. We're going to film you.' Now, why are film directors always so keen to get people into bed?

Actually, the whole session

'Sorry, Bob!'

proved to be quite embarrassing since I really did fall asleep while, around me, the crew were tweaking and twiddling with all their equipment, as these chaps do. This exhausting interlude over, it was back to the course. The evening's lecture on tides was just about to begin. This was meant to be one of Paul's specialities.

No offence to him but, although the lecture he gave was most fascinating, it was also the most intense and detailed. Hearing Paul discussing the effect of the moon on the tides, with their ebbing and flowing, induced a little drifting in me, too.

Paul told us that we'd be learning more about dealing with tides the following day, when we'd be practising launching and handling

Day 3 continued

our Wayfarers. So getting to grips with the direction of the tide and the extent to which its strength varies as you near shallow water was all going to be essential. Mmmm, gripping stuff.

After an hour of this seriousness, we were all bursting for a drink and something to eat. Having missed supper at 7.00, our lunchtime sandwiches seemed a long way away. We leapt into our cars and drove off to the local bistro. A couple of hours later, a very satisfied cast and crew made its way back – slowly – to Plas Menai.

There, we rejoined all the other beginners for a nightcap in the bar. Everyone else, it seemed, had had just as bad a time that day as we'd had – or even worse. Two Wayfarers had capsized, including Tom's; he'd finally had enough, and spent the rest of the afternoon zooming around in one of the rescue boats (he loved that). The other small chap in our group – Job – had been knocked on the head quite badly during a gybing demonstration, and had to be taken off to hospital for a quick checkup, but luckily, the doctors said he was all right. There was unanimous agreement that our hypothermia lecture had come into its own that day.

Despite capsizes, near-concussions and the cold and miserable

> **In some areas of the world, the tidal range can be extremely large. For example, in the bay surrounding the French hilltop abbey of Mont St Michel on the Normandy – Brittany border, the sea goes out about 7½ miles from the shoreline at low tide, leaving behind an immense expanse of sand. When it returns, at great speed, it surrounds the hill, turning it into an island. Something similar also occurs at St Michael's Mount, off Cornwall.**

weather, everyone was still more or less enthusiastic about learning to sail. All, that is, except Tom, who'd decided that, from now on, he'd be an observer, not a participant. Although Mike was naturally disappointed, he did realize that Tom was still a little young to train in a Wayfarer, and as for Tom, he was really looking forward to bouncing along the tops of the waves in the Centre's speedboats.

At last, I made my way to my room. My boots and wetsuit still sat soaking wet in one corner – a real treat for tomorrow morning. I finally crawled into bed, my last thought before falling into a dreamless sleep being a fervent prayer that the weather would improve. If it didn't, maybe I'd join Tom in one of the rescue boats . . .

Tides and tide charts

Tides are caused by the gravitational pull of both the sun and the moon on the oceans of the world. Although the pull of the sun is less than half that of the moon, it is really quite stupendous when you consider how much farther away the sun is than the moon.

The water on the side of the earth facing the sun and moon is attracted outward; oddly enough, this bulging – or high tide – also occurs on the opposite side of the earth at the same time, but the water there is being pushed away. While these bulges are building, low tides occur at the two points on opposite sides of the earth equidistant from where the tidal bulges are at their greatest. Imagine the earth is a clockface: the high tides occur at 12 and 6, and the low tides at 3 and 9.

A rhythm of high and low tides is maintained by the orbiting of the moon around the earth and the earth's own rotation, so that the high-tide bulge and opposing low tide form a wave that passes continuously around the earth. There are two high tides and two low tides during every lunar orbit, but because the moon takes 24 hours 50 minutes to complete each one, the tides will occur progressively later each day.

The gravitational pull is strongest when the sun, moon and earth are aligned in space. The tides that occur then, a couple of days after a new moon and after a full moon, are called *spring tides*. (This name has nothing to do with the season;

rather, it comes from the Old English word *springan*, 'to rise'.) When the sun and moon are at right angles to the the earth – when the moon is in its first and third quarters – the gravitational pull is at its least. These are called *neap tides*. Spring tides are both higher and lower than neap tides.

The difference between a high tide and low one is called the *tidal range*. This can vary a great deal, depending on the marine topography and the shape of the coastline. For instance, on the open sea, the range is no more than a few feet, but in the funnel-shaped

HIGH TIDES				
TODAY	AM	HT	PM	HT
London Bridge	5.43	6.7	6.05	6.3
Aberdeen	5.18	3.4	5.54	3.4
Avonmouth	11.05	11.0	11.13	10.6
Belfast	3.07	3.2	3.41	3.0
Cardiff	10.50	10.3	10.58	9.9
Devonport	9.46	4.6	10.01	4.6
Dover	2.50	6.0	3.19	5.6
Falmouth	9.16	4.4	9.31	4.4
Glasgow	4.22	4.8	5.02	4.5
Harwich	3.39	3.7	4.02	3.3
Holyhead	2.08	4.8	2.42	4.6
Hull	10.17	6.3	10.51	6.1
Ilfracombe	9.53	7.5	10.07	7.2
Leith	6.52	4.6	7.19	4.7
Liverpool	2.56	8.1	3.25	7.8
Lowestoft	1.21	2.3	1.48	2.0
Margate	3.46	4.5	4.10	4.1
Milford Haven	10.13	5.7	10.30	5.5
Newquay	9.09	5.8	9.26	5.6
Oban	9.32	3.0	9.29	3.0
Penzance	8.57	4.6	9.13	4.6
Portland	10.28	1.5	10.28	1.5
Portsmouth	3.14	4.3	3.47	4.0
Shoreham	2.42	5.5	3.15	5.2
Southampton	2.49	4.0	3.21	3.8
Swansea	10.16	8.1	10.31	7.8
Tees	7.49	4.5	8.19	4.5
W'lton-on-Nze	3.36	3.9	3.59	3.5

Tide measured in metres: 1m=3.2808ft.
Times are GMT

Severn Estuary, ranges of as much as 45 feet can occur.

When a tide is changing from high to low, it is said to be 'ebbing'; when it is going from low to high, it is 'flooding'. This change produces a flow of water around the coast, called the *tidal stream*. You can tell in which direction this is flowing by a few simple observations. Boats at anchor will ride on the water with their bows facing into the stream; buoys will lean away from it; a post or other object will have a swirl of water on one side (the direction of the stream). Tidal streams are much faster in deep water and navigation channels, off headlands and during the third and fourth hours of an ebb or flood tide.

The tidal stream can have a great effect on sailing boats. This is even more pronounced when the stream is constricted or obstructed in any way – say, by a headland or a sandbar. This can produce rip tides, eddies and turbulent seas, especially if the wind is blowing in the opposite direction.

Tide tables

What the tides are going to do at any particular time can be discovered by looking at the Admiralty Tide Tables. These will tell you when high and low tides will occur (always expressed in Greenwich Mean Time), and what the range will be (in metres).

Before you go out sailing, you should always check the tide tables to ensure that you will be sailing *with* the tide. That means you should sail out on the ebb tide and sail back on the flood. Say, your boat can sail at a speed of about 4 knots (about 4.6 mph). When you sail with a 2-knot tide, you will in effect be travelling at 6 knots (7 mph); however, if you sail against the same tide, your speed will be reduced to 2 knots (2.3 mph).

Tide tables are usually published in local papers for coastal ports, and they can also be purchased at ship chandlers and at angling and boating shops.

DAY 4

I must have slept like a log. When the alarm went off at eight o'clock, I couldn't believe that it was already morning. The night before, Bob had jokingly said, 'Oh, you'll go to bed and dream about gybing all night.' I'd dreamed of anything *but* sailing!

As I got up, I was acutely reminded of my two days on the ocean's waves: I felt as if I'd been run over by a lorry! Every muscle ached as I stood in front of the mirror counting my bruises. I really drew breath when I saw the ones on my legs, and by this time, my elbow had just got to the mouldy stage. What on earth had I been up to!

I ached my way over to the window to see what treats the day had in store for me. Well, it was pretty grey and dismal, but at least it was calm and the trees weren't trying to leave their roots behind.

We'd have made good exhibits for one of those macabre medical journals as we sat at breakfast comparing bruises, but it would have been difficult convincing anyone that we'd only been sailing (at least, that's how I got *my* bruises . . .).

As Ray and I drifted out into reception, practically everyone we bumped into told us that Bob was looking for us. That could only mean one thing – Trevor! What was it this time?

We raced out to the courtyard, and I think it was the smell that hit us first. Trevor came bounding out to meet us, tugging at the full extent of his chain, tail wagging furiously, tongue lolling

But the principal failing occurred in the sailing,
And the Bellman, perplexed and distressed,
Said he had hoped, at least, when the wind blew due East,
That the ship would not travel due West.

The Hunting of the Snark
Lewis Carroll

Day 4 continued

out, ecstatic at the sight of us and obviously enormously proud of the rather staggering amount of 'presents' he'd managed to deposit in an almost perfect circle around him.

It's hard to be cross with a dog who is so happy to see you. We didn't know whether to laugh or cry, but Trevor thought it was all a new game. Bob, unfortunately, was *not* amused. Even Trevor jumped to attention when he came storming out to tell us that we weren't going sailing until we'd got rid of the mess.

But like the Welsh weather, this particular storm blew over pretty quickly. When we finally made it down to the quayside for the morning's session, we were confronted with the comical spectacle of Bob all togged up in a large, bright yellow sou'wester and a white inflatable ring round his neck with a notice attached that read: 'EMERGENCY BUOYANCY KIT.' Nothing like having confidence in your crew.

Compared to yesterday's near-gale conditions, sailing was a doddle this morning. Mike and I had to launch the boat unaided, and amazingly, everything went according to plan. Once we were underway, we concentrated on gybing. This seemed to take a lot longer to do each time than tacking had yesterday, but as Bob pointed out, this was because we'd done most of our real

tacking then in strong wind.

Now, the thing to remember when you're sailing with the wind behind you is that things start to happen when the sails begin flapping. That's a sure sign that a gybe is imminent: the wind wants to fill the sails on the other side of the boat. Both Mike and I came to know that sign well. Bob had us doing about ten gybes in a row: we'd do one, sail a short way, and then he'd yell, 'Gybe again!' The manoeuvre was really drummed into us, and after a while, we both performed it more or less mechanically.

For some reason, Mike was again finding it difficult to take things gently, and now his great problem was keeping his balance. He really had to concentrate on just keeping calm and learning to sail sensitively. We made a good pair because we could bolster each other's confidence when either of us was in trouble; now, even though we were battered and bruised and every movement was agony, we were feeling much more confident.

Opposite
Don't forget the boat's tied to the trailer!

Day 4 continued

Day 4 continued

The morning passed quickly and soon it was time for our mid-morning coffee break. We made for a small cove and stopped near the shore.

When we were ready to set off again, Bob hopped out. 'You two stay right where you are. I'm abandoning ship! You're on your own now!'

'Are you ready for this, Mike?' I asked. I personally wasn't too worried. When I'd first heard that I'd have to 'go solo' during this course, I'd had a moment of panic, imagining being left to my own devices with no one to turn to. But, in fact, going solo in a Wayfarer just means sailing without your instructor – so it was Mike and me on our own.

'When you're out there,' said Bob, 'you have to think "What point of sailing are we on? Which course are we sailing? Where should the sails be?" When you go downwind, you have to be

sure to let the sails out, and when you're sailing into the wind, you need to be close-hauled.

'So,' he continued, 'where's the wind coming from?' I pointed. 'Right. So where are you going to sail?'

'We should pick a spot over towards those houses on the other side of the Strait.' I pointed again, this time to a village of stone-built houses on the opposite bank.

'Which house?'

This seemed a bit too specific, but I replied, 'The pink one? Mike's favourite colour!'

'Fine.' Bob got out of the boat and squatted in the water beside us. 'Now, Annie, I want you to sail out as far as that little headland – no further – and then come back towards the shore here. Do that two or three times, and then hand over to Mike. If you're not happy, come back here. Don't worry – I'll be in the

The first modern offshore (or ocean) yacht race was held in 1866. Two wealthy men, angry at an article in a New York newspaper that criticized local yachtsmen for not venturing beyond the sheltered waters of the Hudson River and Long Island Sound, decided to race their yachts – *Vesta* and *Fleetwing* – across the Atlantic in the middle of winter. To add spice to the event, they bet each other $30,000 – a fabulous sum in those days.

When 25-year-old Gordon Bennett Jr (who later sent Stanley to Africa to search for Livingstone, and from whose name we get the mild expletive) heard about the race – and the bet – he challenged the other two to let him and his yacht, the *Henrietta*, enter. They agreed, subject to him also putting up

Day 4 continued

rescue boat.'

Going solo was a bit like leaving home for the first time: it took Mike and me some time to sort everything out. As the sails flapped in the wind, all the ropes mysteriously lost their identities, and as we pulled away, my last memory was of Bob screaming out, 'Don't forget to put your rudder down!'

Once out in the Strait, however, everything I'd been taught and all the manoeuvres I'd practised again and again came back to me. In addition, the boat, now minus Bob's weight, handled like a dream. I felt a great rush of

Going solo

Day 4 continued

confidence, and began to enjoy sailing for its own sake.

Bob came zipping up beside us in the rescue boat. 'How does it feel?' he shouted over the noise of the motor and the gusting of the wind.

'Wonderful!' I yelled back. 'We miss you desperately! Got no one to shout at!'

'Well, in that case, I'll go back to the Centre,' Bob bellowed with a grin.

'No, no, you hang around,' Mike and I chorused, then tacked away from him.

After I'd been back and forth across the Strait three or four times, Bob shouted for us to change places. Sailing at full speed, this wasn't easy. Mike stretched his left arm right round my back until he could grab the tiller and mainsheet I was holding, while at the same time, I had to take the jibsheet from him with my free hand. Then he slid

down the side of the boat towards the stern, while I shuffled carefully the other way to take up his former position. Now it was Mike's turn to show what he was made of, and he did brilliantly. We were definitely the dynamic duo that morning.

Finally, Bob told us to turn back to the shore where we'd started. Once we'd brought the boat in and made it secure, Mike and I fell into each other's arms in triumph. It was a great moment, and even more amazing when you think that we'd done all that after such a short period of training – one of the joys of sailing!

Bob was very pleased with us, but we realized that all we'd achieved during the previous hour had simply been an extension of what he'd taught us so thoroughly. We were keen to get out on the water again and happy to leave Bob behind – 'Besides,

$30,000. In the end, it was Bennett who got to England first and pocketed $60,000, but he would have won even if the *Henrietta* had come in last: the other two men had kept to their sheltered waters and allowed their yachts and crews to brave the winter gales without them.

Opposite
Learning about the triangular course

Day 4 continued

not to be personal, Bob, but you were beginning to get in the way!'

We sailed back to Plas Menai, me at the helm and Mike crewing, and on the way, I had another wonderful experience. Bob yelled, 'Gybe!' from the rescue boat. Before, whenever he'd given me an instruction, I'd taken at least ten seconds just to work it all out mentally. Now, for the first time, I did it without thinking. It was a thrilling moment – perhaps not everyone's idea of a terrific experience but it was to me!

Back at the Centre, as we were all eating our sandwiches on the quayside, Bob told us about the next hurdle we were to attempt after lunch: the triangular course. Three buoys were placed in the middle of the Strait, and the idea was to sail around them. Mike and I were at a *slight* disadvantage here. The rest of the class had spent much of the previous gusty day trying to go round the course;

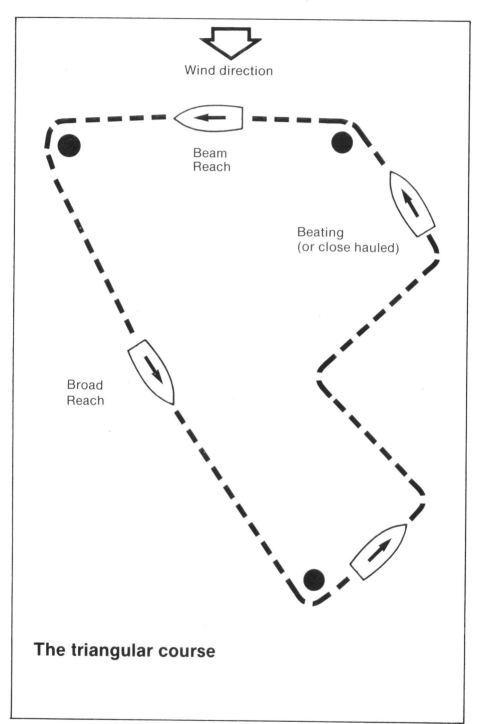

Wind direction

Beam
Reach

Beating
(or close hauled)

Broad
Reach

The triangular course

Day 4 continued

they'd been shown diagrams of the best way to tackle it; and they'd also gone over the course again with their instructors that morning. Because of the filming, Mike and I hadn't done any of that – although, given the disaster that followed, I have a sneaking suspicion that our director rather fancied the idea of us being led like lambs to the slaughter. He was not disappointed.

As we began the first leg, Mike and I soon discovered two things: (1) we hadn't a clue which way round we were supposed to go; and (2) we didn't know how to deal with all the problems as they arose. Not only did we have to go round the buoys successfully, we also had to watch out for everyone else – and they, despite all their training, seemed to be having as much trouble as we were!

The problem with negotiating a triangular course (see diagram) is that, as you're continually changing the direction of the boat as you steer towards and round the buoys, you have to make frantic adjustments to the sails and centreboard to cope with the wind hitting you from various angles. And this happens every few seconds – it was exhausting.

Looking back, I can see why a triangular course is useful; it makes you put everything you've learned into rather urgent practice. We were supposed to sail into the wind, close-hauled, to-

wards the first buoy; once round this, we had to bear away, slacking the sails a little on a beam reach to get to the second one. Then we were to steer round through a broad reach, with our centreboard halfway up, to get near the third buoy. By the time we did, we should be practically running, with the centreboard fully up, ready to gybe round the buoy. After the gybe, we had to steer back into the wind, pulling in the sails so we'd be in our original close-hauled state ready to strike the right angle to reach the first buoy again. (I hope you're paying attention to all this!)

Well, that's the triangular course in *theory*! I'm afraid that it didn't go exactly according to plan . . .

I took the helm first, and after about ten circuits of the course, I was finally beginning to crack it. Then it was Mike's turn to be captain. Right on cue, it suddenly became really gusty – poor Mike. But he persevered, and just as he was getting the hang of it, we were distracted by our director yelling at us: 'Over here now, and sail over the top of me!'

Now, that may sound a bit strange, but Mike had got so used to the weird and wonderful ways of film folk that he obeyed immediately, aiming the boat as best he could towards the place where our director, kitted out in wet suit, mask, fins and snorkel, was treading water with an underwater camera in his hand.

Being an expert sailor, his request was quite a simple matter to him. To us, however, who'd only just figured out how to get around that wretched course, it was the most complicated thing he could have asked. It totally threw Mike.

The events of the next few minutes seemed to occur in slow motion. I watched Mike's face change . . . the sails change . . . . the worried faces of the film crew . . . as the inevitable happened and we gracefully keeled over.

There followed about half an

Our director calls us over

'Is it a tack or a gybe, do you
think, Annie?'

'Neither, it's a capsize!'

Day 4 continued

hour of hysterics. Why capsizing should have this effect on me, I don't know. I think it was the sight of Mike grappling around up to his neck in water, glasses still on his nose, thinking of his nice, warm, cosy job back home . . .

I was faced with my usual problem of trying to clamber on to the centreboard; this was a feat in itself, covered as I was with so many bruises. When I finally made it up, I leaned back, pulling on the jibsheet to right the boat, but my boots never seemed to get a grip and I kept slipping off. I tried valiantly twice, but in the end, Paul had to come to my rescue. He hopped casually on to the centreboard from one of the rescue boats and pulled our Wayfarer up with just his little finger. It was most depressing.

Mike and I were now very cold and very tired. In fact, of all of us on the course, Tom seemed to be having the most fun, flying over the water in one of the rescue

Opposite
Tom in the rescue boat

'Just stop laughing and get on with it!'

Day 4 continued

The weather and sailing

Nowadays, what with weather satellites, television weather maps with computer graphics, and news of weather disasters in all the media, it's almost impossible not to know at least something about how weather works.

Before you even consider going out on the water, you should make sure that you have a good idea of what weather is expected in the area, how it will affect your sailing and even whether you should be going out at all. However, most of the weather reports we receive on radio or television are far too general to be of much use to the dinghy sailor.

The most obvious source for weather reports are the shipping forecasts from the Met Office, broadcast on BBC Radio 4. You can catch these at 05.55, 13.55 and 17.50 every day, following any gale warnings that may be in force. Each broadcast is in three parts: first, a general synopsis of the weather for all seas surrounding the British Isles; then, detailed forecasts for each of the shipping areas; and, finally, reports from coastal stations. The forecasts are given in a kind of shorthand, but include predicted wind direction and strength, weather and visibility, while the coastal reports give actual wind, weather conditions and barometric pressure for certain places.

Probably of least use are the inshore waters forecasts, which predict weather conditions for the seas within 12 miles of the coast – they are much too general. Again

these are broadcast by BBC Radio: at 00.38 on Radio 4 following the shipping forecast, and at 06.55 on Radio 3.

However, because of lack of time, these national radio forecasts tend to be cursory. For fuller information, you could try ringing Marinecall, the special recorded telephone service for yachting folk. In addition, if you're near a major seaside town, it's always a good idea to listen to local radio: some stations give detailed local weather forecasts.

If you hear that the winds in the area in which you plan to sail are quite gusty, you can go out with your mainsail already reefed. If windy weather is predicted, you will be forewarned and prepared to reef if necessary. As a beginner, however, you should be cautious about sailing in bad weather – after your training, your instructor or a rescue boat won't be with you in case you get into trouble.

If you're keen to become more qualified as a sailor, the Royal Yachting Association's Level 3 course includes a section on simple meteorology. This covers: sources of information, such as radio and TV programmes, shipping forecasts, local forecasts (weather centres) and newspapers; simple interpretation of a synoptic chart; the main characteristics of high-and low-pressure areas; the significance of rapid and continuous changes in barometric pressure; awareness of changing weather conditions; and the Beaufort wind scale.

Day 4 continued

boats, sticking out his tongue at us. Mike and I decided to call it a day and, after sailing back to the Plas Menai slipway and securing the boat, dripped our way back to the Centre and straight upstairs to our rooms for hot showers.

That night's lecture was all about that great British obsession – the weather. Paul explained to us that weather is created by the combined forces of pressures and fronts. High pressure comes from the tropics and low pressure from the poles. I wasn't surprised to learn that good old Britain is in a relatively low pressure area: the *polar front*, where the warm air of the tropics meets the cold air of the poles. The warm air rises and the cold air forces its way underneath. If the warm air falls again as it cools, the pressure will rise and there should be clear skies. However, if the pressure falls, expect rain. It was a pretty depressing lecture all round, particularly when Paul started analysing the weather we were having at the time.

Obviously, it's crucial to check weather reports before you go sailing each day, and there are various methods of getting this information: the newspapers, the radio shipping forecasts and, particularly, Marinecall. This last will give you an update of the weather on your particular bit of coastline. It even tells you the state and temperature of the sea – useful for people who have succeeded in turning capsizing into an art form.

We were scheduled to go out on a cruise the following day, and this, Paul told us, was when our lectures and sailing experience should all come together. As he sent us off to buy him a drink at the bar, he said that he expected us to be able to give him a clear picture of the tides and weather first thing in the morning.

What'll yours be, Mike? Double brandy?

Life on the ocean waves can have contradictory effects. It has been clearly demonstrated that a life at sea can have profoundly beneficial results for maladjusted, educationally backward, wayward or delinquent young people. However, a study a few years ago showed that 12 per cent of all seamen suffered from neurotic illnesses – much more than any other occupational group!

The Beaufort Scale of wind force

Beaufort number	Description	Speed (mph)	Sea state
0	Calm	Less than 1	Sea is mirror-smooth.
1	Light air	1–3	Small wavelets like scales; no crests.
2	Light breeze	4–7	Small wavelets, still short but more pronounced. Crests glassy and do not break.
3	Gentle breeze	8–12	Large wavelets. Crests begin to break. Foam is glassy.
Novice sailors should not venture out in the following			
4	Moderate breeze	13–18	Small waves becoming longer; 'white horses' more frequent.
5	Fresh breeze	19–24	Moderate waves, longer; many 'white horses'.
6	Strong breeze	25–31	Large waves beginning to form; white crests more extensive.
7	Near gale	32–38	Sea heaps up; white foam blown in streaks.
8	Gale	39–46	Moderately high waves of greater length; crests begin to form spindrift. Foam blown in well-marked streaks.
9	Strong gale	47–54	High waves; dense streaks of foam. Crests begin to roll over.
10	Storm	55–63	Very high waves with long, overhanging crests. Surface of sea is white with great patches of foam. Visibility affected.
11	Violent storm	64–73	Exceptionally high waves. Sea completely covered with foam.
12	Hurricane	74+	Air is filled with spray. Visibility seriously affected.

DAY 5

Thursday was cruise day. I woke very early and flung back the curtains to make my own weather forecast. The sea was dawn-calm, the sky a gentle pink. With a day like today, I could even enjoy my bruises, now entering an interesting orange phase.

For once, I was famished, and I actually had some breakfast. (It always surprises me that life goes on at this time of day.) The same conversation was bubbling over everywhere. Did anyone know where we were going on this cruise? Had anyone listened to the early shipping forecast on the radio? We'd all had such good intentions the night before. I'd set my radio alarm for 5.55 am to catch the forecast on Radio 4, but I'd hit the 'off' button after just a few seconds; at that time of the morning, I was in no mood to hear about Dogger, Fisher or German Bight.

I went off with the film crew to ring Marinecall. The voice over the telephone confirmed what we'd all hoped: 'There are no gale warnings in operation for sea areas Irish Sea and Malin. Maximum daytime air temperature: 18 degrees Celsius. Sea temperature: 14 degrees Celsius. Sea state: moderate.' I breathed a sigh of relief. Everything was going to be fine; the good sunny weather was going to hold all day.

Down at the quayside, which was bathed in deliciously warm sunshine again, everyone in the class seemed to have shed the last vestiges of the depression that had spread the day before,

The smaller the vessel, the more likely those on it will suffer from seasickness. During the first two or three days of an Atlantic crossing, approximately 25–30 per cent of all passengers on an ocean liner will become seasick. However, this will happen to 60 per cent of the occupants of inflatable life rafts.

Seasickness is an indication that the organs of balance in the inner ear are in good working order: if they were not, you would not become seasick. If you do, take heart – Lord Nelson suffered regularly from *mal de mer* and was still able to win the odd sea battle.

Day 5 continued

after the disastrous triangular course, and it was smiles and grins all round. Not only because of the lovely weather but also because, with the cruise, we now had a real purpose to our day. It was like a school outing!

However, although I was looking forward to the cruise, I was still worried about how we would do today; Mike and I had suffered a bad blow to our confidence. Still, my partner seemed as cheerful as the rest of the class, and in a flash of great optimism and 'Isn't life wonderful?', we both decided not to wear our waterproofs.

While Mike was away from the boat for a few minutes, hunting up Tom, I prepared a surprise for him. Carefully wrapping a bottle of champagne and two glasses in my waterproofs, I stashed them away in the bow of the boat, praying silently that we wouldn't capsize.

Paul called us together to brief us on the cruise. He had a large chart propped up against the mast of one of the Wayfarers, and after we decided which way the tide was running – which determined which way we would sail – he showed us where we would be going; up the Menai Strait beyond Bangor, to a pub called the Gazelle. He then described the details shown on the chart – where the deep water was, which places should be avoided because they became too shallow when the tide went out and so on – as well as where the buoys were in the channel and what various ones meant.

Opposite
'Come on, Mike, gently does it. You've only got two more days with her!'

Charts

All charts are based on a grid system. The latitude is printed on both the side margins, and the longitude on the top and bottom, and there are lines extending from each edge to form the grid. The latitude is measured in degrees, which are divided into 60ths or 'minutes' of latitude. A minute is equal to the distance of one nautical mile (6080 feet). While the measurement of latitude remains constant, the distances between the lines of longitude - or *meridians* - do not. This is because the meridians eventually converge on the North and South Poles, and so, whereas the

Day 5 continued

distance between two lines of longitude is 60 miles at the Equator, this dwindles to nothing at either pole.

The different depths of water in a given area - or *soundings* - are also shown on a chart. These are expressed in metres (or, on some older charts, in fathoms - 1 fathom= 6 feet), and are measured from what is known as the 'lowest astro-nomical tide', or LAT; this is a theoretical measurement, much lower than any normal low tide. Soundings that are underlined - e.g. 6 - indicate *drying heights*. Rocks and sandbanks may be covered at high water but reappear at low tide, and the height above the water that these hazards achieve is expressed as so many metres above LAT.

Day 5 continued

From the general to the particular; Paul then showed us the place on the chart where we would encounter the only real hazard of the cruise. This was The Swellies, a strangely named group of rocks just beyond the Britannia Railway Bridge, where the water swells in large rapids into a sort of whirlpool. (I later heard that The Swellies can be particularly lethal when the wind is a bit strong and the tide is running in the wrong direction.) Paul thought we weren't ready to tackle them on our own, and so we'd have to be towed through when we got there.

We wouldn't be sailing up the Strait on our own. Paul, Bob and

Opposite

No venturing into uncharted waters for us

the other instructors would be accompanying us in two rescue boats equipped with walkie-talkies linked to the Centre. The main rescue boat – a huge, old wooden motorboat called the *Angharad* – would be taking the film crew and everyone's packed lunches, thermos flasks and spare waterproofs. All pretty well taken care of, one way and another.

The sun was still blazing as we rigged the boat, all on our own for the first time. On our first day of training, Bob had helped us, and as we got more proficient, he'd simply make comments from outside the boat. In addition, the class helped each other, often coming over and demonstrating a particular knot or whatever. One class member, another Bob, had a different technique: we'd ask him a question such as 'Where does this rope go?' and he'd reply, 'I'm not being rude, but frankly, you should work it out

show small areas of the sea and include a great amount of detail. For most dinghy sailors, a large-scale chart of the area in which

You can purchase charts that are small, medium or large scale: small-scale charts cover vast areas of the sea and are of use only to those undertaking ocean cruises; large-scale charts, on the other hand,

they are going to sail – plus, possibly, charts for areas nearby where they might be forced to sail in the event of bad weather – is all that is necessary.

Your chart will give you information about any useful land features as well as details about the coastline, seabed, anchorages, aids to navigation and warnings of special

Day 5 continued

Day 5 continued

for yourselves. You'll remember that way.' Visions of Kenneth Kendal . . .

Today, everything seemed to be cooperating fully, every rope, knot and sail sliding effortlessly into position. Mike and I looked at each other – 'Right, we're in complete control. We know exactly what we're doing.' He was dashing around so efficiently at his end of the boat that I decided to leave him to it. 'See you later, Mike – let me know when you're finished.' I walked off to a wail of *'Mummy!'* This team was inseparable!

It was odd how everything fell into place. On the first day of the course, when Bob had shown us

Opposite
In complete control?

how to rig the Wayfarer, it had all seemed so haphazard and unsystematic – as if someone in a really filthy mood had decided on a rigging method that would completely floor novices for generations. But now, four days into the course, we could understand what the various bits and pieces did; we'd think it through and work out which rope and clip was doing what. It was really all very straightforward, wasn't it, we asked each other.

That's what we thought . . . There we were, waiting proudly beside our boat for Bob's inspection, sure that we would pass with flying colours. Then, when he did inspect our handiwork, he found something that we hadn't done quite right. Nothing vital – not a matter of life and death – just the way we'd stowed one of the ropes. This was a hard man to please.

Paul had gathered us together

dangers such as rocks, wrecks, eddies and tidal rips. No coastline is static – there are always changes in contour (above and below the water) and in the placing of lights, buoys, etc. Therefore, it is imperative that you buy the most current chart available, and make sure that you update this frequently with the relevant Admiralty Chart corrections – called 'Notices to Mariners' – which are available at chart dealers.

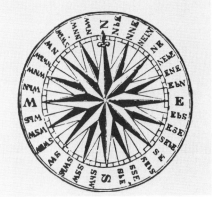

Day 5 continued

on the quayside for one last briefing before we set out. 'We need a lead boat,' he said, 'one that the rest of you will follow down the Strait.' He looked at the four Wayfarers, their rigging swaying in the light breeze. Now came the moment of truth: 'Right, Annie and Mike, I want you to be the lead boat.'

Oh no! Mike and I looked at each other, and I could tell that he was as close to panic as I was. There was no way that we were capable enough to lead anyone – we had enough trouble simply staying upright!

We were saved from revealing our true colours in the nick of time. 'Oh, no, sorry, I made a mistake,' said Paul. 'I meant that boat there' – and he pointed to another one with an orange stripe on the top of the mainsail. 'The lead boat is usually the one with the sail that's slightly different from everyone else's.'

Mike and I went limp with relief, and silently thanked all the gods that be for giving us a boat without an orange flash on the top. With all this lengthy preparation, anyone would think we were setting off up the Amazon!

That just left us with one problem: Trevor. First thing in the morning, Bob had made it abundantly clear to Ray that Trevor wasn't to be left to 'enjoy' himself in the yard like yesterday, and he wasn't to be left within barking distance of the Centre. Now, we couldn't leave him locked up in the car, so what were we to do with him? In the end, we tied him up as far out of sight and hearing as possible, and felt very guilty leaving him there.

At last, we got underway, tacking off from the slipway with me at the helm, Mike pushing us off and deftly jumping in at the last minute. Tom had decided to join us today, but only as a passenger.

Perhaps the most famous Wayfarer is *Wanderer*, which was owned and sailed by Frank and Margaret Dye. In it, they made journeys from Scotland to Iceland, the Faeroes, Norway and the Arctic Circle, as well as many day trips around the coast of Britain. In 1976, after totting up an amazing 40,000 miles during 19 years of cruising, *Wanderer* was given the unique honour of being the first Wayfarer to be given a place at the National Maritime Museum in Greenwich.

Buoys and transits

When you are sailing, it is important to have some idea of navigation, and particularly where it is safe for you to be. Your charts will help you to do this, but you must also keep an eye out for markings on the sea and land – that is, buoys and transits.

Buoys come in a number of colours and shapes – flat-topped cans, conical, round, or with either a vertical structure or a spar on top – and some also carry lights on top. What each buoy means can vary depending on which part of the world you are in, but the buoyage system in use around the British Isles is the Maritime Buoyage System A, which comprises cardinal and lateral marks.

Buoys that are cardinal marks indicate compass directions and denote the position of dangers; thus, depending on the cardinal mark, your boat should remain to the south, north, east or west of that particular buoy. Lateral marks, on the other hand, tell the person at the helm to stay on one side or the other of the buoy, to avoid danger. In combination, cardinal and lateral marks show the locations of channels, estuaries, harbour entrances, etc. Buoys are also marked on charts.

In general, buoyage systems are relevant only to those sailing in large vessels. In fact, dinghy sailors may find it safer to sail *outside* marked shipping channels; the water will probably still be deep enough and ships will be avoided. However, attention should always be paid to buoys marking specific dangers.

Transits, too, can be very useful when piloting your boat. A transit is formed when two specific objects are lined up; the imaginary line running through these is then the one to be followed. A transit can comprise two lights that, when lined up, act as a guide into a harbour; alternatively, you may be told to keep one headland clear of another to avoid hidden rocks. Particularly with the latter, less formal type of transit, you should check the direction of the transit with a compass and compare this bearing with the one marked on your chart (or perhaps with any local sailing directions you have been given), to make sure that you have identified the correct objects to be used.

Day 5 continued

The cruise

Day 5 continued

Although he seemed, on the face of it, quite confident, after the bad capsize he'd experienced two days before, he'd lost his nerve. 'You're not going to gybe, are you?' he begged. 'You promise you're not going to gybe?' But on that cruise up the Menai Strait, he had nothing to worry about – we were in complete control.

It should have been plain sailing from then on, but loud barking made me look back. Sure enough – it was good old Trevor, broken loose from his tether. I yelled out to Ray, who was in one of the rescue boats, and we all chorused out to Trevor to quiet down. But this was quite a difficult concept to put over to a dog who was obviously aching to join us. No matter how much we waved our hands at him to tell him to go back, Trevor got more and more excited, and in the end, he leapt into the water and propelled himself over to Ray's boat, using his tail like an outboard motor! So Trevor came, too.

Conditions were perfect. The joy of being in a boat with friends on a glorious, sunny day! The feeling of control and independence as you catch the wind in your sails and rustle through the water, the sun gently warming your back . . .

In fact, the wind was so light that, for the first hour or two, we hardly moved at all – some of the others even brought out their paddles to speed things up a bit! – and this gave us a chance to consolidate everything we'd learned. Still, every time we went beyond a snail's pace, Tom threatened to jump overboard and swim for shore: 'Don't gybe – whatever you do!'

Soon, however, the glorious weather and the lovely scenery we were passing affected even Tom. For the first time, we all had an opportunity to soak up our surroundings. Before, they'd either been shrouded in mist or we'd been too busy trying to prevent the boat from keeling over to notice them. Today, as we sailed between beautiful green hills on either side, we kept coming across surprising hidden inlets and lovely little cottages down on the beach. This really did seem to be what sailing was all about. Mike and I decided that we could cope with this speed (or lack of it) for the rest of our lives – it was so peaceful.

Tom's one obsession is bird-watching, and here in the Strait, there were plenty of birds to see. Back at the Centre, when the rest of us would be comparing notes on rigging or some other

Opposite
Tom, Mike and I enjoying our picnic at Bangor

105

truly nautical subject, Tom would say, 'Oh, I saw a curlew' or whatever species had been hanging around the boats that day. Even in the middle of an outdoor lecture or a capsize, he'd call out, 'Wow! Look at that guillemot!'

As well as the cottages, the shore was dotted with beautiful stately homes. One I recognized instantly: 'That's Plas Newydd, the home of the Marquess of Anglesey.' I'd actually landed by helicopter in the back garden,

Plas Newydd

By the shore of the Menai Strait, beyond a sweeping lawn, is Plas Newydd, the stately home of the Marquess of Anglesey, where Victoria spent the summer before her coronation. It achieved its present appearance in the first decade of the 19th century, when it was rebuilt by British architects James Wyatt and Joseph Potter, in the then-popular Gothic style.

The estate is now owned by the National Trust, and the house and gardens are open to the public. Among its attractions are a small military museum, and the huge mural of ships, sea and mountains painted on one of the dining room walls by Rex Whistler between 1936 and 1940.

Day 5 continued

but it seemed a bit over the top to mention it at the time.

We broke out into 'Didn't We Have a Lovely Time the Day We Went to Bangor'. As our voices pealed over the water, Bob whizzed up to us in the rescue boat.

Not one to miss out on a chance to teach us, especially not in these tame wind conditions, he told us to practise 'boat trim'. This meant that, with some skilful and cunning shifting of our weight to the back, or aft, of the

The first Marquess of Anglesey was Henry Paget, who was second in command to Wellington, and in charge of the Allied cavalry, at the Battle of Waterloo. It was there that he was severely injured, resulting in the nickname 'One Leg', but this didn't hamper his career for he later was appointed Lord Lieutenant of Ireland.

A short way up the coast from Plas Newydd is the 90-foot-high Marquess of Anglesey's Column, raised in 1816 in honour of Henry Paget (his statue was added to the summit 44 years later). Those with enough stamina can climb up the more than 100 steps inside the column; once at the top, there are splendid views of the Menai Strait, Anglesey and the mountains of Snowdonia on the Welsh mainland.

Day 5 continued

boat, Mike and I could make the Wayfarer go a bit faster. Also, by leaning hard over to one side, we were able to capture more wind in our mainsail, which was already fully extended as we were sailing with the wind behind us.

We were going great guns, overtaking the others, until they all began to catch on to what we were doing, and their instructors began to shout some coaching to them from the *Angharad*. It was amazing how competitive Mike and I felt. We were only going on a short trip up the Strait, but we all had the determination of any Fastnet sailor as, hell-bent, we tried to gain on the lead boat. I can see how sailing can really get into your blood.

Then we hit The Swellies and had to stop. We felt we'd been doing so well that it was a bit humiliating to resort to being towed, but Paul and Bob insisted: there was so little wind and the current was so strong that we'd have gone round in circles. Soon we were linked together by our painters, and the *Angharad* pulled us through the cross-currents.

It took rather a long time to get through, but all in all, we made good progress. After we sailed under the stunning Menai suspension road bridge, its central span looming above us, we soon spotted the Gazelle on the left bank and headed in to land.

Our first attempt at beaching was brilliant, absolutely no problems, but the film crew were way behind us, covering everyone sailing into the little harbour together. They needed a close-up of Mike and me landing, so out we went again. By this time, all the other boats had already come in, and there was very little room left to 'park'. Our second landing was, of course, stunning: we thudded straight into the stern of another boat in great style!

The Atlantic may have been crossed by Irish monks in their round leather coracles well before Christopher Columbus ever got the idea, but in modern, *documented* times, it was not until 1866 that any small sailing boat made this perilous voyage. The successful craft was a 26-foot iron lifeboat called *Red, White and Blue*, which sailed from New York to Deal in Kent.

Opposite, above
'Where's the wind?'

Opposite
Coming home the easy way

108

Day 5 continued

Day 5 continued

And, of course, *this* was the one that was captured on film for posterity, and was watched with great interest by the legion of elderly gentlemen lined up on the stone wall in front of the pub sipping their pints.

Still, we weren't the only lunchtime entertainment. Sandy and her son James proved the theory about irresistible forces meeting immovable objects when they crashed noisily into a metal buoy. ('Noisy' being the operative

The bridges of the Menai Strait

Prior to the construction of the Menai Strait bridges, people had no choice but to sail or swim to and from the Welsh mainland. In fact, between the 15th and 18th cen-

turies, more than 3000 head of cattle swam across from Anglesey each year, guided by drovers. The building of a bridge was first suggested in 1785, but this and other proposals were turned down after protests from the ferry owners about loss of earnings and from ship owners because of possible interference with navigation through

Day 5 continued

word – we could hear them argu-
ing about whose fault it was
from across the bay!) And, inci-
dentally, this answered that question of mine: why the instructors
at Plas Menai try to separate
members of the same families on
these courses!

We were moored (finally) in
one of the prettiest little harbours
that I'd ever seen. Beyond the old
wall above us was the Gazelle, a
lovely, old hotel. There was just
one little lane running down to it
from the hills behind, but on that
sunny day, it had attracted sailors
and tourists from all around, who
were sitting on or leaning against
the little wall that ran down to
the hotel's own jetty. The day
was so superb, the setting so
perfect, that I couldn't have
chosen a better moment to produce the champagne. To Mike's
amazement, I fished out the
bottle and glasses, which had
miraculously survived intact.

'What's that, Dad?' asked Tom
as his father began to open the
bottle.

'It's your actual Moët,' Mike
replied, twisting the wire from
the cork.

'*Mould?*' Tom squeaked in dis-
belief.

'It's like fizzy lemonade,' I con-
tributed. 'Hey, there's Bob,' and I
waved for him to join us.

As we dug into our plastic bags
to get at our sandwiches, we
filled Bob in on our journey – or,
rather, voyage – to the Gazelle.
'Even Thomas, our passenger,
enjoyed himself today, and was
very good company,' said Mike,
obviously relieved that Tom's sea
legs had returned, even if he is
only a fair-weather sailor!

However, even at this idyllic
picnic-spot, there was no peace
for the wicked: Paul decided that
the day wouldn't be complete
without another lecture, just to
remind us that we were on a

the Strait.

Then it was decided to build a
road that would run between
London and Holyhead (on Holy
Island, separated from Anglesey by
a narrow channel); from there,
traffic could continue by boat to
the Irish port of Dun Laoghaire.
However, without a bridge over the
Menai Strait, the scheme would
come to nothing.

Enter Scottish engineer Thomas
Telford, one of the brightest stars
of the Industrial Revolution. He had
already had a plan for a cast-iron
arched bridge over the Strait turned
down in 1811, but then the Admiralty
saw his design for a suspension
bridge at Runcorn in Cheshire. This
was never built, but the Admiralty

Paul's lecture

liked the design so much that they asked Telford to build a similar one over the Strait, to be the final link in the London - Holyhead road (now the A5).

Work got underway in 1819, and six years later, the elegant Menai Suspension Bridge was finished, at a cost of £120,000. Constructed of stone and wrought iron, it is 1265 feet long with a 579-foot central span, 100 feet above high water. By making it this high, Telford pleased the ship owners, for the bridge allowed even the tallest sailing ships to pass beneath it unhindered. (The ferry owners were never placated.) Originally fitted with four massive iron chains, these were replaced with two steel ones when

Day 5 continued

course. We all sat on the ground in a circle round him to be briefed on the journey home. It would be much choppier as the wind had got up a bit, and we'd be fighting the wind, even though the tide was on the turn. (Tom made an instantaneous executive decision to ride back in one of the rescue boats.) Because of this, it was quite likely that, as we followed each other in a crocodile, we'd keep running into each other, and it was important for us to know who had the right of way.

This is called the 'Rules of the Road'. I'd always thought that there was an unalterable law about who had the right of way on the water: power gives way to sail. That is, if you are in a tiny dinghy and a ship approaches you, the ship has to give way. And that sailing boats automatically give each other right of way as a courtesy. But not so – there's a whole list of laws of sailing protocol (*see below*). Paul soon put me right.

'Rules of the road'

- Power gives way to sail in open water.
- Power gives way to sail at all times if the 'power' is a small motor-boat.
- Sail gives way to power when large ships are in restricted shipping channels.
- If one sailing boat heads directly towards another – called being 'on opposite tacks' – the one on a starboard tack (with the wind blowing on to the right, or starboard, side) will have the right of way over one on a port tack.
- If two sailing boats are travelling on similar courses that look like converging, the one furthest from the wind – the leeward boat – has the right of way over the one closest to the wind (the windward boat).
- If your boat has right of way, you must maintain your course.

all the metal of the bridge was changed to steel in 1938-40, to strengthen it. Today, the bridge is immortalized in the 'suspension bridge motif' knitted into sweaters on Anglesey!

Although now linked to the mainland by road, the people of Anglesey soon came to realize that they were missing out on the great rail revolu-tion. Who better to solve their problem than engineer Robert Stephenson, son of George, father of the locomotive and inventor of the *Rocket*?

Choosing a spot to the south-west of Telford's bridge, in 1846 Stephenson began the construction of the five towers that would sup-port the two 1500-foot-long rectan-

Day 5 continued

The power-giving-way-to-sail law only applies in the open water. In rivers, estuaries and in places like the Menai Strait, big ships have to keep to the dredged channels. If you get in their way and they have to turn to avoid you, they could run aground. Besides, huge ships like oil tankers can often take miles to come to a halt.

Paul drew the outline of a ship on the pad of paper he was holding; then he added a dot next to the ship. 'This,' he said, pointing to the dot, 'is a dinghy. Who do you think is going to give way?'

We all laughed, and I remembered my encounter with the tanker.

'But you're right in one way, Anneka. Small powerboats do have to give way to sail at all times, because it's easy for them to stop and change course.'

Then Paul ran through the rest of the Rules of the Road –

that is, who had right of way between sailing boats – which was to prove very good advice for our homeward journey.

After about an hour and a half, and a lot of a chat and a bit of sunbathing, we set off for Plas Menai. Despite the wind being against us, we made good progress, occasionally being buzzed by the rescue boat containing a cheeky Tom. However, when we reached The Swellies, there was no question that we could get through on our own, so all of us made for the shore and took down our mainsails. The *Angharad* did the honours again, and in a long queue, we were tugged over the turbulent water. When we'd left The Swellies behind, we untied our painters, raised our sails and continued under wind-power.

It was great sailing weather and the best sailing we'd had all week, and on the journey back,

gular tubes through which the trains would travel, also at a height of 100 feet above high water. These tubes were made of wrought-iron plates weighing a total of 10,000 tons, and each was floated into position on a pontoon, then raised by a hydraulic press in the 230-foot Britannia Tower. In 1850, the bridge, now christened the Britannia Railway Bridge and costing £600,000, was opened. It was decorated with lions sculpted by John Thomas, who was also responsible for the stone decoration on the Houses of Parliament.

Day 5 continued

'Can't we just stay here all day?'

In 1970, a fire seriously damaged the bridge, which had to be closed for two years for repairs. When it reopened, the famous tubes were gone, replaced with open track and light steel arches. And over the track was now a roadway, needed to cope with the increasing traffic that was clogging the Menai Bridge.

Both these bridges are justly famous and much photographed. However, sailing beneath them gives a unique opportunity to examine their construction and marvel at the inventiveness of Telford and Stephenson.

Day 5 continued

we were able to do a lot of filming. At one stage, Digby climbed aboard to get some shots of us on the boat. This was more difficult than it sounds, considering how impossibly long Digby's legs are. He'd be precariously perched at the front of the boat, balancing the heavy camera on his shoulder and leaning over at a dangerous angle, when we'd put a quick tack in and he'd be nearly catapulted over the other side. We didn't know what to grab first – Digby or the camera. Professionalism triumphed, I'm afraid (sorry, Digby).

Meanwhile, Mike and I had made a complete breakthrough: we just gybed and tacked without thinking. Before then, our sailing had been done on a very structured learning basis, but now we were simply playing around, catching the wind and turning this way and that – whichever way our fancy took us. By the time we arrived at Plas Menai, burned by the sun, full of champagne and laughing our heads off, we were totally exhilarated by the whole experience.

Bob was waiting at the slipway, watching our final approach. From the expression on his face, I could tell that he was pleased with us: he'd been able to see that, for the first time, we'd really been sailing in the fullest sense of the word. As he helped us de-rig the boat, he said that he was chuffed that we'd managed to do so much – and this despite all the sailing time we'd lost because of the filming. We'd not had nearly as much chance as the others on the course to practise and practise, but we'd caught on anyway.

That night, the Centre held a barbecue. Tomorrow was to be our last day, and this was a chance for everyone to get together – people from the other courses

You become eligible for the exclusive **Ocean Cruising Club** if you can prove that you've cruised under sail for 1000 nautical miles without putting into port.

Opposite
Plas Menai catering: the barbeque and 'school dinners'!

Day 5 continued

Day 5 continued

that we hadn't seen all week, such as the mountaineers and canoists, as well as all the staff. We were quite a crowd. A disco had been set up in the games room, which was packed with gyrating 10-year-olds. Where had they all come from?

Sitting there, our plates piled high, we rediscovered our bruises – or, rather, mine. It was ridiculous – but then someone only has to nudge me and I'm scarred for life! I had well over 80 by this stage.

'What happened to "man overboard"?' I asked Bob as I sat down next to him. 'Does this mean that we don't have to do it?' That morning, before Paul had shown us the chart and described our journey to the Gazelle, he'd taken us through what to expect during the 'man overboard' exercise: when we'd have to throw a plastic bottle attached to a bailing bucket (the 'man') off the boat and then retrieve it. However, because we'd had such a long, leisurely lunch, we hadn't had time to perform this important life-saving technique on the way back to the Centre.

'Oh, no,' said Bob, 'that comes tomorrow. Do you remember when I came up alongside you in the rescue boat and asked you to turn the boat up in to the wind, try stopping it and then turn away again?'

'No!' I said.

'Well, that was in preparation for the "man overboard". Once you can do that, that tells us that you've got "boat control". And you'll also feel satisfaction because it means that you can go away from an object, turn around, come back and stop in exactly the right place.'

I found it hard to believe that Mike and I would achieve that degree of expertise by tomorrow. Tacking and gybing were one thing; stopping dead on target was something completely different.

'So what else will we be doing tomorrow? Our last day.' I did feel pretty gloomy about the prospect of leaving.

'Well, first thing tomorrow morning,' Bob replied with a strange smile, 'I'm going to show you how to work a trapeze!'

'Sure,' I said, 'and I'll bring along my sequinned leotard . . .' (Funny, I didn't think he was that kind of chap . . .)

Opposite above
The barbeque

Opposite
Blackboard instruction for the 'man overboard' drill

118

Day 5 continued

DAY 6

'Ready about! . . . Lee oh! . . . Stand by to gybe! . . . Ready! . . . Gybe oh!'

Again and again, I tacked and gybed up and down the Menai Strait, feeling the strain as I braced myself and pulled in the mainsail. There was only one thing I didn't understand: why didn't I have any clothes on? Then in the middle of a particularly tricky manoeuvre, I woke up.

It was still very early – only 6.00 am – but I got up anyway, inhaling sharply at the aches in every part of my body. I was exhausted, but my spirits lifted as I threw open the curtains and saw that it was absolutely lovely, a rosy sky with just a few soft, plump clouds. Maybe this was the day I was going to pick up my healthy yachtsman's tan.

I knew that I should try to get

some more sleep – as it was my last day at Plas Menai, I wanted to be in a fit state to do everything on offer – but the prospect of sailing in such wonderful weather was so exhilaratinging that I only managed to sleep for half an hour before my alarm went at 8.00. When I opened my eyes this time, I found that British summertime had triumphed yet again: the sun had gone, and the Strait was shrouded in mist.

When the class had assembled downstairs, we were told by our instructors that we should reef our mainsails before we even set off – an ominous note. When we'd rigged the boats and pulled

Opposite
The picnic at Bangor
Overleaf
Such progress – in less than a week

Catamarans

Typical single-hull sailing dinghies rely on their width, or *beam*, to give them stability in the water – the wider across they are, the more stable. However, a dinghy that is quite wide (and, therefore, quite stable) is harder to sail through the water than one with a slim hull, simply because it's fatter. A catamaran – a light sailing vessel with two slim hulls connected by two cross-beams – achieves greater stability without the drag of a large hull surface, and can sail much faster than a dinghy of the same size.

Catamarans were used for centuries by the Polynesians of the

Day 6 continued

It looked beautiful at sunrise . . .

Opposite
**Robert White, a Hurricane –
and me**

**. . . but not so good by the
time we got out there**

Day 6 continued

the trolleys down to the slipway, we could see that it really was very gusty and the water was quite choppy. Paul and the other instructors said they reckoned that many of us were going to end up capsizing again. Silently, we looked at each other, our pale faces reflecting our thoughts: *What a way to finish the holiday . . .*

Mike and I were pretty miserable. Yesterday we'd ended the day confident and optimistic, as if we were Olympic-class yachtsmen, but now our confidence had gone with the sun.

Bob said that he was seriously considering cancelling the morning session. About half of the class yelled, 'Yippee!' but the rest of us looked a bit sad because, after all, it was our last day and we'd wanted to make the most of it. In the end, however, ambition outstripped caution and, intrepid as ever, six of us decided to brave the seas.

It was the right decision. After a few hairy moments, when gusts threatened to flatten all three boats, the weather settled down and the sun came out. In fact, it was probably the nicest conditions we'd had all week, particularly after all our training: gusty enough to make it challenging and sunny enough to make it appealing.

First, Mike and I decided to tackle the triangular course again. Since our last fatal attempt, the fact that we'd not really done it properly had rankled, and we were determined to complete it brilliantly before the end of the course. And so we did. This time, every manoeuvre suddenly made a lot of sense, and after our journey into the unknown the day before, sailing round the three sides of a triangle seemed quite straightforward and, moreover, it was fun. And this time, we didn't capsize – the world was

South Pacific to travel the long distances between islands. Built of local materials, they were virtually two boats held together by two cross-beams - in fact, 'catamaran' derives from the Tamil words for 'tied logs'. Topped by thatched huts, the larger ones looked like floating villages, but breath-takingly speedy proas were also used. These have one main hull with a rudder at either end, and one much smaller hull called an 'outrigger' for stability. To tack, the rigging has to be reversed and the proa steered from the other end.

Catamarans appeared surprisingly early in Europe. They were introduced by the eccentric Sir William Petty, an Irish baronet, who built waiting, but we coped all right.

Now for the 'man overboard' exercise. Bob came up alongside us in the rescue boat to coach us, step by step. After Mike threw our 'man' – an empty plastic bottle attached to a plastic bucket – into the water, we had to turn into a beam reach and travel – rather perversely – about 50 yards away from the 'man'. Then we had to come back on the same beam reach tack, but this time with the jib loose, flapping wildly in the wind. The reason for this is, if you genuinely do have a man overboard, then that's your crew gone. Also you travel more slowly with the jib in this power-less, flapping state.

Now came the tricky bit: trying to judge at what point to turn the boat towards the 'man', and releasing the mainsail at exactly the same moment. Hopefully, you come to a complete standstill in this 'hove-to' position, able to

lean over and retrieve your poor, half-drowned crew. That was the 'man overboard' exercise in *principle*, but when I carried it out on my own (Mike theoretically didn't exist since he was supposed to be in the water), I found it difficult to estimate the speed of approach.

Still, I managed it perfectly first go, but – as usual – Sod's Law prevailed: the film crew were changing batteries at the time and didn't catch the golden moment. And could I do it again? I must have gone through the whole procedure four or five times before I finally performed it to the film crew's satisfaction.

It was quite complicated. There was our director in the water with his underwater camera, trying to get bow-wave shots and close-ups of the 'man' while I was trying to retrieve it. There was the crew filming from the stationary rescue boat, and I had to make sure that I tacked as

three of them between 1662 and 1664. Another - called the *Experiment* - was built and sailed in 1664 but, while it successfully achieved the crossing to Portugal, it sank in a storm in the Bay of Biscay as it tried to return to England.

This seems to have ended any popularity that the catamaran might have had, for it wasn't until the

1870s that the American boat designer Nathaniel Herreshoff built six of them. Twenty years later, a Canadian-designed catamaran representing the Royal St Lawrence Yacht Club won every race it entered at a competition. Rather than impressing the other yachtsmen, the powers-that-be of the sailing world banned catamarans from

Day 6 continued

Day 6 continued

close to them as possible.

Finally, everyone was happy – the film crew, me and the 'man' – and Mike and I settled down for a splendid and invigorating sail back to Plas Menai and lunch.

The world did look good that morning. The only black cloud on the horizon was a figurative one: this was my last sail with Mike. We'd gone through so much together that week, espe-

Opposite
Rescuing our 'man'

Toppers

competition! Catamaran sailing did not officially resurface until the 1930s.

After the Second World War, the development of new boat-building materials that were both light and cheap put new life into the multihull movement. By the mid-1950s, enthusiasts were lashing together racing canoes in the Essex marshes,

building 40-foot catamarans in Hawaii, and sailing across the Atlantic in plywood vessels built in haylofts for £200.

As the 1960s approached, there was an explosion in multihull design and building, although the more conservative-minded at the yachting clubs rejected the whole concept. Soon there were small

Day 6 continued

cially all the traumas with the filming. Mike certainly hadn't been expecting to deal with that when he and Tom had happily set out from Macclesfield last Sunday for a week's sailing.

All too soon, we were mooring at the Plas Menai slipway and heading back to the Centre. For our last afternoon, we were all down on the main notice board for 'Sailing Other Craft'. I wasn't sure quite how much say we had in what 'Other Craft' we were going to be trying our hand at, but I'd been eyeing the little single-handed Toppers with dread. Not once had the Topper class returned looking anything but drenched through, and I really didn't fancy ending my week with a soaking like that. I'd rather got my eye on the elegant, Mediterranean-type cruiser yachts, the Sonatas, and started lobbying Bob over lunch to see if Mike and I couldn't have a go on one of

those. Much more my style!

But Bob wasn't moved by my blandishments, and with an evil look in his eye, he told me that he wasn't going to let me get away *that* easily – oh, no. He wouldn't explain what he meant, and only told me to wait and see. I was definitely being set up for something here, and the knowing looks and grins from the film crew only served to deepen my suspicions . . . *Come on, guys, what's going on?*

Finally, Bob led me to his office and handed me a complicated harness. He told me to put it on as quickly as possible as he had to dash downstairs to hand out all our dinghy sailing certificates. Then he disappeared, and I was left to puzzle it all out on my own. As I struggled into the harness, I consoled myself with the thought that at least I hadn't seen any Topper sailors wearing anything that remotely resembled this.

catamarans used primarily for messing about on the water, racing catamarans, catamarans for cruising and large catamarans for ocean-crossing races.

Catamarans finally got some official approval when they dominated the 1959 *Yachting* magazine regatta in Miami. Out of this competition arose the International Catamaran Challenge Trophy – commonly known as the 'Little America's Cup' – which was first held in 1961. Since then, the world of multihull racing has expanded – for instance, in 1974 Robin Knox-Johnston and Gerry Boxall won the Round Britain Race in a 70-foot catamaran – as has the number of new designs, not least of which are

Day 6 continued

Finally, I was ready to join the class, intent on finding *somebody* who might let me know what was happening. Surely Mike . . .?

Everyone in the class was making their way to the quayside, ready to tackle the Toppers and Sonatas. First, however, Bob gathered us together for an impromptu awards ceremony. Everyone got one – even the youngest, Tom and Job, received RYA Junior 1 Certificates, which meant that they had learned the basic skills of boat handling, while the rest of us were awarded RYA

the Tornados and Hurricanes of Reg White and his son Rob. And today, catamarans and the other multihulls - proas and the three-hulled trimarans - have achieved the recognition they deserve, both from the official yachting organizations and from the sailing public.

The reward at the end of the week. Bob hands out the proficiency certificates

Day 6 continued

National Dinghy Sailing Certificates (as of 1988, this course will be called RYA Award Level 2).

One by one, Bob handed the certificates out: 'David . . . Bob . . . Sandy . . . James, *despite* demolishing the post . . . Tom, who's had a great week . . . Mike, who's endured more than he thought he was coming for . . .' Then it was my turn, but Bob held on to my certificate. 'If you could possibly wait, Anneka, I have something I want to show you that will blow your mind!'

Everyone seemed to be in on this joke except me – even Mike. With Bob steering me, I staggered down the slipway (I could barely stand up straight within the confines of the harness).

'I thought you were ready for something a little faster,' said Bob.

There, at the end of the slipway, was a sight of blue, mauve and pink magnificence, straining and lashing over massive twin hulls. Bursting to tear off across the water, it looked like something out of a glossy Martini advertisement. This was excitement. The word 'HURRICANE' blazing across the sails left me in no doubt as to its power.

Bob introduced me to this magnificent beast's owner, Rob White, European and World

'She's mad to go out on that'

Day 6 continued

Tornado Champion. I later found out that his father, Reg White, had won an Olympic gold medal in 1976 for sailing a Tornado catamaran, and that both father and son are world famous – not only for their nautical achievements but also for designing and manufacturing catamarans. The Hurricane now before me in all its glory was their latest model.

Now, it seemed, Rob was going to teach me how to sail this! He showed me how to attach myself to the boat: a line extending from the mast down to one of the catamaran's hulls had a clip on it that I attached to the harness I was wearing. I was to be sus-

pended over the side, my weight held by the line and my feet on the hull giving me the only stability I had. This was the 'trapeze', and I was the afternoon's circus entertainment.

Rob didn't exactly stand on ceremony. One moment I was gingerly testing my clip technique; the next, we were flung into the middle of the Menai Strait. The wind caught the sails of the Hurricane so quickly that it was like being catapulted from the slipway; compared to the Way-

'Over to you, Rob, she's a nutcase!'

Day 6 continued

farer, the speed was breathtaking. I hung, suspended in mid-air, as the boat sliced through the Strait, spraying us with water, and the hull I was standing on leapt several feet so that the catamaran stood right up on its side. I think it was the most exhilarating thing I've ever done. (I know I *always* say that – but it *was* great!)

The way Rob kept control at that speed seemed remarkable,

and yet, in a funny way, the Hurricane seemed a lot more stable – and was a lot more comfortable – than a Wayfarer. This must be due to its construction: in a catamaran, you are cushioned from the water by the two hulls,

'Look, are you sure about this?'

A final briefing from
Robert . . .

. . . and away we go

Day 6 continued

whereas in a typical sailing boat, there is only thin planking between you and the water, and you feel the pitch of every single wave. We skimmed across the surface of the sea.

The 'deck' of the Hurricane was a piece of canvas stretched tight between the two hulls. Because it's so bouncy, it's called the 'trampoline', and it was so comfortable that, if the wind hadn't been gusting and we hadn't been hanging off the edge parallel to the water, we could have sunbathed on it.

At one stage, Digby came aboard with his camera; this was attached by a cable to the rescue boat, which Bob was steering with amazing dexterity. Rob and I had to make sure that we sailed as close as possible to the rescue boat, while Digby, prancing about

on the trampoline and constantly flung about and drenched with spray, somehow had to stay on the catamaran. But he did get some spectacular shots.

Later, when Digby was filming us from the rescue boat, Rob decided to show what the Hurricane could do. Suddenly the hull under our feet was standing almost vertically out of the water and the sails were nearly skimming the waves. As for Rob and I, we were lying out on our trapezes, hanging parallel to the water.

I was really chuffed when Rob gave me a go at the helm. To my amazement, although the techniques for tacking and pulling in the ropes did vary slightly, I found that I could transfer the same principles that I'd learned on the Wayfarer to this very different boat. For example, if you find that you are going too fast and you're going to tip over, you just release the sail a bit, steer the boat away from the wind and lose speed instantly – just like in the Wayfarer. The Hurricane was manoeuvrable and controllable, even for a beginner like me, and I had a great feeling of power, of being totally in control. In fact, I found that a lot of things were easier than they had been on the Wayfarer.

Not that everything was a piece of cake: being at the helm could be really hairy. You have to switch sides when you tack, just like on a Wayfarer, but instead of just moving to the other side holding the tiller and mainsheet, on a catamaran you have to unhook yourself from the trapeze and try to scramble across the trampoline at the same time. If you make any kind of sudden movement, you start to go in the wrong direction or put the wrong strain on the ropes. I came a cropper a couple of times, and hung from the trapeze wondering how I was ever going to survive! Luckily, Rob was able to extricate me relatively painlessly, and on the whole, he was really pleased that I took to it so quickly.

Everything happened so fast. I'd gybe or tack, scramble across the boat, steer round, hook myself up, push myself out; then because we were moving across the Strait so quickly, we had to repeat the whole process just seconds later. Pulling the jibsheet was also very hard work – it required a lot more strength than it had on the Wayfarer – and I really had to strain every muscle. Even so, I couldn't always pull in the ropes enough to go the speed that Rob wanted. He would casually lean over and, with one hand, yank the sail in another few inches. I was suitably impressed.

Towards the end of the day, my hands were feeling arthritic from the strain of holding the jibsheet so tightly, and I'd collected some new bruises on the backs of my thighs from the jolt of sitting in and out of the trapeze. (By now, the bruise count must have reached the 100 mark.) My face was also very sunburned, which was extraordinary since the sun certainly didn't feel that hot, and I was absolutely exhausted, my eyes glazing over with tiredness.

All these things were forgotten when Rob would say, 'OK, turn now' and just presumed that I knew how; he didn't say, 'Now, you remember how to tack, don't you?' which was the process we'd gone through all week. And I *did* know how, I *did* know when it would be best to gybe or tack, finding the wind, making constant adjustments. For the first time, I knew that I was sailing really well – a wonderful way to end the week.

There was quite a band of spectators watching us from the shore. It must have been a beautiful sight; the Hurricane's multi-coloured sails and the boat skimming the surface of the waves at an alarming angle. I brought the boat into the Plas Menai slipway where some of my classmates were still waiting, and jumped off and waded to shore.

Shedding my harness, I grabbed Mike – who didn't need to be asked twice – and within seconds, he was up and away, and soon

was just a tiny speck on the horizon. I'm so glad that he enjoyed it as much as I did – it's not every day that a beginner gets a chance to sail a Hurricane with a world-class sailor. Maybe he'll forgive me now.

As I staggered up to the Centre, I took one final look at the Strait, shimmering now in the setting sun. The Plas Menai boats swung slowly at their moorings, promising more adventure, joy, despair and fun for the next lot of students who would be lucky enough to come here to learn to sail.

Everyone on the course with me got something out of it – even Tom, who did more riding around in rescue boats than actual sailing

138

Day 6 continued

– and they all said that they'd be recommending it to other members of their families and their friends.

As for me, I found that I took to sailing more naturally than to any other sport I've tried. There is something about the freedom and sheer exhilaration of moving over the water with the wind at your command that adds a wonderful new dimension to life. Maybe it was the salt water in my British blood, but as I prepared to leave Plas Menai, I knew that I would be sailing again – and soon!

Postscript

But I didn't know it would be *that* soon . . .

Less than a month later, I was with the *Wish You Were Here* team in the United States, at Myrtle Beach, South Carolina. They were going to film me sailing off in a Hobie Cat – a small catamaran – along with a bronzed beach bum. Once the crew set up on the beach, we had just ten minutes to do the whole sequence – after all, they were only after a dramatic sailing-off-into-the-sunset shot. Anyway, off we went.

Day 6 continued

All was going well, the sun was beating down, wind in my hair, spray on my face, etc., etc., when a real-life drama unfolded. A boat had capsized miles out at sea and its crew were unable to right it (memories of me and Mike at Plas Menai!) – and there were *sharks* circling them! We immediately set off to the rescue. (Did I hear the *Hawaii Five-O* theme tune soaring above the swell or was it just my imagination?)

We reached the capsized boat, and my hunky partner *dived off* our Hobie to help the panic-stricken victims. That was where the script let me down. I was now sailing solo for real – not Plas Menai solo, but *solo*! I could actually see white sharks swimming under the twin hulls of my catamaran, and all I could think of was that my film crew, miles away back on shore, weren't going to record the final curtain . . .

Somehow – and we may never know how – I made it back to shore in one piece. There I found the film crew blissfully unaware of my ordeal, and anxious to move on to our next location!